# AWAKENING
# YOUR
# *Creative* VOICE

## Women in a World of Possibility

## ELSIE RITZENHEIN

MASON WORKS PRESS

BOULDER, COLORADO

*Awakening Your Creative Voice:*
*Women in a World of Possibility*

For information, please contact Kathy Mason, Publisher,
at kathy@masonworksmarketing.com,
or write to Mason Works Press,
6525 Gunpark Dr. #370-426, Boulder, CO 80301.

Disclaimer: While the publisher and author have used their best efforts
in preparing this book, they make no representations or warranties
with respect to its accuracy or completeness.
In addition, this book contains no legal or medical advice;
please consult a licensed professional if appropriate.

Cover and Interior Design by Kathy Mason and Jennifer Thomas-Hayes
Cover photo by Rob Ritzenhein

ISBN: 978-0-9983209-0-8  (Softcover)
First Edition
Library of Congress Control Number: On file

Published in the United States of America
Printed in the United States of America

# PRAISE FOR *AWAKENING YOUR CREATIVE VOICE*

"One of the greatest misconceptions of all time is the belief that being fruitful and multiplying, along with creating, is reserved for a woman's ability give birth. The desire to create, not simply procreate, is encoded into our Divine Human Blueprint. Creation is the driving force behind our individual and collective evolution as is the desire to be fruitful with our gifts and multiply them for the greater good of humanity."

—Victoria Reynolds, Author, Speaker, and Thought Leader

"Creativity is an essential skill for the 21st century. As the feminine spirit comes into balance on the world stage, the creative aspect of 21st century living is necessary for us all. *Awakening Your Creative Voice* is a clarion call to all women (and men) to start exercising their creative muscle in the new stewardship (leadership) for our coming world."

—Brian Luke Seaward, Ph.D., Author of *Stand Like Mountain, Flow Like Water* and *Stressed Is Desserts Spelled Backward*

"*Awakening your Creative Voice* by Elsie Ritzenhein quickens our inventive spirit, points us to the natural state of being and reveals the possibilities of space consciousness from which artistry arises. She encourages us to take the 'risk seat' and supports us by suggested inquiries into the essential questions that lead us to discover the 'Playground' of the Creative Self. An imaginative and resourceful guide for an inspired journey!"

—Victoria Friedman,
Co-Founder of Vistar Foundation (www.vistarfoundation.org),
Author of *Spirit Doodling: The Effortless Expression of the No-Mind*

"While reading *Awakening Your Creative Voice,* Elsie Ritzenhein became my hero. As an innovator and leader in the field of education for over fifty-two years, her pioneering voice vibrates throughout each page, inspiring us to grab the opportunities available to us as women at this time of great change and to choose to be powerful, creative leaders. She implores us to risk, to no longer be good girls, to use our voices. She then takes us by the hand and shows us how to do all the above. I recommend you read this book as a roadmap to shift your own life, and then buy a copy for your daughter—and your mom. I promise they'll thank you."

—Debra Poneman, Bestselling Author,
Founder of Yes to Success Seminars,
Co-Founder of Your Year of Miracles Mentoring Program for Women

"This is the era for women whose creativity, intuition, and courage are leading the way to our future. Elsie Ritzenhein's new book, *Awakening Your Creative Voice,* guides the reader towards remarkable possibilities for those who discover their creative voice. In her book, Elsie offers support on the journey of overcoming challenges, discovering one's own values, and creating new ideas for an empowered future ahead. A must-read for all modern women."

—Monika Burwise, Co-founder of Global Awakening Institute

"Elsie Ritzenhein brings her extraordinary insight and experience to this rich, delightful, and inspiring work on the intuitive, creative, and visionary power of the feminine. A must-read for women of all ages who deeply care about their essential role as leaders, teachers, and conscious creators."

—Sharron Rose, Filmmaker, Author of *The Path of the Priestess*

"This is a nurturing book—a visionary practicum. In the world of often harsh or glib advice of quick-fix methods, this book holds safe and sound space for the emergence of your voice. To the experienced leader, it is an offering, an invitation and a refreshing reminder. To the emerging leader, it is a generous guide for stepping up to the self and into the world with graceful power. Elsie Ritzenhein outlines an ecology of leadership that aims not just to sustain us but lead us to thriving. Nurturing creativity is and will be the measure of our true progress and evolution and of the new leadership that envisions it. This book is one such great envisioning and the voice of its author the great invoker of your own powers within. I truly hope you answer this call."

—Mila Popovich, Ph.D., Founder of EvolvED Leadership Chair, Membership Communications Committee, World Academy of Art and Science

"This book captures Elsie's life, work, careers, learning, physical and emotional journeys, along with her many relationships and what each of them has gifted her as part of her whole being.... Her evolution over time and space and place is captured in this book that she's birthed. With this work, she's pulled every learning, emotion, truth, and toolkit to give to all of us. It is full. It is rich. It is a bible for the mind, body, and spirit. Those who read it will benefit—if not from the whole—from the pieces that 'sing' to them. And that is what matters."

—Leslie Wilson, CEO, One-to-One Institute

*The voice of my grandmother said to me,*
*Teach your children what you have been taught.*

—Brother Eagle, Sister Sky:
*A Message from Chief Seattle*

*For Rob, Rachel, Levi, Maebel, and Edith,*
*my love to you forever.*

*For Stephanie,*
*who helped me know what I must do.*

*For Great-Grandma Sarah Ann Hixenbaugh,*
*whose spirit lives inside of me.*

# CONTENTS

*May the sun bring you*
*new energy by day,*
*May the moon softly restore*
*you by night,*
*May the rain wash away*
*your worries,*
*May the breeze blow new*
*strength into your being,*
*May you walk gently through*
*the world and know its*
*beauty all the days*
*of your life.*

—Apache Blessing

# PREFACE

*F*or the first time in history, women are in the position to excel as creative leaders in the world. Released from previous constraints, you are free to fly…to be powerful, to shape our future through your unleashed creativity. We have waited lifetimes to be present in this space with each other. You are emerging in a world of infinite possibility. This is a world where we can embrace our hearts and souls along with our minds—where we become truly alive and truly creative. Your capacity and skills have never been more important.

There is great change happening in the universe, and in the midst of this change we need to challenge either/or assumptions, understand and embrace unity consciousness, generate new stories and think differently. We need to be radically creative and courageous, and we need to focus on being aware of our natural creativity by engaging all of our senses—including our intuition. Women have a unique role in creating the future, and our internal and external power is especially meaningful. Your creative voice, your values and your exciting new ideas are more than significant for our progress.

Taking up this challenge requires transformation from within— from inside, from the Self. Change can happen in no other way. Our willingness to question and act from a place separate from our assumptions and deep mental models—as well as outside our constraints and our continuous experimentation with the same-old-same-old that keeps us stuck in the tar pit of the status quo— means acknowledging and accepting our innate creativity. Alone and together, we create to embody shared meaning for our organizations and our culture. We create networks that are always interconnected. We co-create for the renewed future of our world. From your love, inner intelligence and imagination, you bring unusual and exciting talent to our world.

Being a creator means claiming—or reclaiming—who you are. It is a process of emergence and awareness, of allowance and acceptance, of joy and celebration. It is a knowing—a return to your heart and your soul. Being a creator means moving forward with all your glory and abundance. Your unique role for creating the future is rich, authentic and powerful. Creativity is your birthright and your purpose. I know that you belong in the space of possibility. The purpose of this book is to help you open your heart and move forward with courage and enthusiasm.

# INTRODUCTION

## The Voice

*There is a voice inside of you*
*That whispers all day long,*
*"I feel that this is right for me,*
*I know that this is wrong."*
*No teacher, preacher, parent, friend*
*Or wise man can decide*
*What's right for you—just listen to*
*The voice that speaks inside.*

—Shel Silverstein

*A*ll of us have a voice that speaks inside. Mine is eager to share with you what I've come to know about creativity and creative leadership, and about the creative spirit that lives in each of us as we maneuver in a world of global complexity. Your voice as a woman is especially pertinent and valuable in our world. I'd like to offer some perspectives from my experience that I believe will be useful and exciting for you as you develop your creativity muscle and grow as a creative leader.

I grew up in a much slower world than we have now, as a member of what we call the Silent Generation. I was born between the GI Generation and the Baby Boomers. This time was a bridge between the reality of WW II, the return of our fathers who served in the war and a life of recovering and building. We experienced rationing during the war only to have it followed by enormous economic growth. For me, growth happened overnight. I remember that the pasture just across the alley and the street from where my mother and I lived when my dad was in France and Germany turned overnight into a community of cheaply built homes. In 1945 my father came home from the war, and my twin sisters were born a year later on my birthday. My dad expanded the little house to hold the larger family and built a garage on the back of the property next to his ample garden. His beagle hunting dogs slept in the pen attached to the garage, and we had a couple of good-sized pet rabbits for a while. I lived there until I was married at twenty-one.

Growing up, I was a rigidly compliant, achievement-oriented, outwardly focused young woman. Until I was twelve years old, the paddle was used in my home, and I knew the daily fear of not doing as I was told. In many ways, I didn't have a voice that spoke out loud. When I left for college I knew that when I graduated I wouldn't come back to my home town to live. The voice that spoke inside of me back then seemed to be clear and strong. It developed more clearly during my years at the university, and I've learned to follow it all my life, sometimes hesitantly, but always to where I needed to be in the end.

In 1965, after graduating from college, I married and left home and began teaching music. Around 1993, my twenty-eighth year as a teacher, consultant and educational leader, I happened to read Margaret Wheatley's new book *Leadership and the New Science* (1992). From that pivotal moment my perspective about leadership in education changed. Around the same time, I also read *Making Connections/ Teaching and the Human Brain* (1991) by Renate Nummela Caine and Geoffrey Caine. As a result, my entire professional life felt validated. Other people saw the world as I was experiencing it! I was standing HERE, and someone else got it. All of those years of teaching and leading seemed to matter, including my beliefs about learning and creativity. The Caines's research and perspectives helped shape my understanding of the role of research in the new field of neuroscience and learning. After reading those two books, I became devoted for many, many years to perspectives anchored in knowledge about generativity, living systems, complexity, creativity, interconnectedness, and holistic perspectives related to personal and professional growth that were anchored in what we were beginning to learn about the brain. Today, as an educator and educational leader through a career that has spanned fifty-two years so far, I find myself as enthusiastic about creativity and leadership and as compelled to want to contribute as I was at the beginning.

The voices that move me, now and in the past, include those of authors, great teachers, artists of all disciplines, my maternal grandmother, my paternal great-grandmother, my son and some valued friends, family and colleagues. I have invisible allies that have strong and powerful voices. Here are some ideas that have shaped my thinking and my work over the years and have led to this book:

Jean Houston (*The Wizard of Us,* 2012*)*, Joseph Jaworski (*The Source*, 2012), Meg Wheatley and the Caines tell us in a variety of ways about butterfly time, a generative, creative order where we live on the edge of creating new ideas, and about an underlying guiding intelligence in the universe that prepares us for futures that *we* must create.

In a book titled *Generative Leadership: Shaping New Futures for Today's Schools* (2008), which was co-written with authors Karl Klimek and Dr. Kathryn Sullivan, we talk about generativity as a capacity to create, to produce and to give rise to new possibilities and new constructs. Learning, thinking and acting generatively means understanding the system in which we live and work, as well as our individual living system as a human being. Moreover, generativity embodies emergence, co-creation, and being open, empowered and dynamic. It's a natural influence within the unified field.

I am especially moved by Clarissa Pincola Estés, who, in *Women Who Run With the Wolves* (1992), writes so eloquently about women and creativity and our need to find and capture our innate femininity.

This is a really exciting time for me, because I know that change is here and it's happening fast and furiously. This change and the questions that exist in the universe that challenge our very way of being are the container for *why* I believe creativity is so very crucial for you and me. As individuals and leaders we often speak of creativity and innovation but do little to allow creative energy to emerge. It has been and is still a command-and-control world within organizations and a testing and accounting world in our schools. We've been working in the factories of our businesses and our schools for a century or more, and we've learned to believe that this is what the world must be: everyone toes the line and watches the clock. If we do this, we'll be rewarded. My experiences have led me to believe that we're broader and bigger than the roles we play in this paradigm that we've experienced. Creativity is, in fact, our very essence. All of us are

born with and hold throughout our lives the energy to be creative—
to fulfill possibilities. We can choose to be creative and to be leaders.
Now is the time to live this reality. We don't need to rely any longer
on an old, broken system that isn't working.

I *must* write this book. I know this, and I'm pleased to be aware
of the voices inside of me that tell me to begin—and to finish. My
hope is that this book helps you think, feel, respond and act in ways
that will bring creativity and creative leadership to your life. I want to
share for women who are ready for creative perspectives and practices
at a time of fundamental change in our universe. My professional
arena for work and growth was education. The experiences I share
and examples I give you come from my years in that field. Since all
of you have been through the educational system, I'm guessing you'll
understand what I've written about. Your arena may be healthcare,
business, non-profit, the trades, parenting, technology. You may
be a graduate student or a student just beginning your advanced
education. Whatever you do and wherever you are, this information
will hopefully be exciting and useful for you. I'll offer some of my
experiences, my thoughts and beliefs, some experiences and thoughts
of favorite authors, friends and colleagues, as well as some ideas for
action for you and your world.

My best hope is that you can see and feel the energetic, creative
spirit that has appeared to me and that this spirit influences and ignites
a light within you. I've had a creative life from my beginning and
continue to have one every day. You have one, as well, but you must
be willing to find it and connect. I hope you'll have the desire and
incentive to come along and to share what you learn and experience.
We have very important work to do.

—*Elsie Ritzenhein*

All that you do
is important.

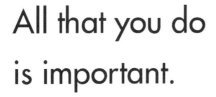

You *become*—
then you *act*.

Your creative life

*matters.*

CHAPTER 1

# WHAT
# MATTERS?

*"Awareness always precedes progress."*

—Kim Cary,
Tai Chi Teacher

## AWARENESS MATTERS

*A*wareness *of your creative being matters.* Creativity and creative leadership aren't magic acts that come only to a few for your special work and recognition. They can't be bought in a store or ordered online. Creativity is who you are: inside, outside and all around the town. Your individuality, friendship, thinking, working and parenting are important. But your creativity is what matters most in the universe. *Creativity is about looking at the world in a different way. Awareness is about broadening that focus and perspective…and is a good place to start.*

Your personal world and your professional world are both in the mix. First, you become aware of yourself as a living system and a creative being—as a resilient, intelligent, self-renewing woman—who is more open and more powerful than you may have thought. Then you begin to see how you interact with the world, independently and without direction, and what you can do differently as you co-create with others and with the larger system. Co-creating means participating in the evolution of the universe by being receptive, positive, thoughtful, joyful—and active. As a living system you hold the universal energy that comes to you for observing, exploring, reflecting, incubating ideas, processing, designing, improvising, meditating, conversing, noticing, listening and balancing feminine and masculine perspectives that are unique to you as a human being. As a woman, you embody sensitive, nurturing, gentle feminine energy that holds and develops ideas until they birth, so that you can respond imaginatively, compassionately and with personal power to disturbances in your environment. It's this rich, vibrational, massive field of energy and the capacity for using it to be creative that makes you so special and that is so critical for leading now and into the future.

Tapping into this energy and allowing it to emerge means that you manifest your personal power into your environment as thoughts, beliefs and actions. You allow your innovative and entrepreneurial impulses to emerge and expand to whatever your imagination can see and feel. This phenomenon is holistic and happens in all aspects of your life, individually and collectively. The energy is literally ever-present. Becoming aware of its existence, its power and its potential for possibility is the very foundation of your work as a creative woman and leader. Giving birth to ideas and new constructs is what all of us, both women and men, need to do in this time of instability, revolution and renaissance. Your contributions are essential to the flow of rich interactions and interdependence that are natural to life and that should be natural in our homes, schools and organizations. Used compassionately and creatively, your self-discovery, voice and awareness of the system all lead to an exquisite influence that disturbs and disrupts so that new contexts emerge from the continuous shift that's happening.

The energy that you share in group gatherings, meetings, classrooms, department stores, work environments—the field of energy, the place of interconnectedness, the source of our capacity to access knowledge for action—influences thinking and behavior in ways that you may not have learned to recognize because of our mechanistic, cause-effect environments. Harnessing and enabling this potent source of creativity can be found especially through being silent, being in the moment and becoming aware, and being present with your intuition and cognitive knowledge combined. From a still and silent place you act with resolve and bravado to what Madisyn Taylor calls "…the pure energy of creation." (2008, p.100) This source can also be found collectively through dialogue with others as partners and in groups such as the circle. It's the energy that provides strength for your inner and outer life and for your wisdom voice. It moves you to be more than you might have thought you could ever be.

Once you've found this center for yourself, how can you consciously take it to work? How can you begin to be aware of the need for dialogue about energy and creativity that doesn't frighten everyone, especially when it's linked to leadership? How can you create a mind-shift for yourself and with others around a perspective about energy in our culture that has been labeled "woo-woo," so that you can acknowledge and explore uniqueness? How do you talk about what you *feel* along with what you *think*? About intuition along with strategic plans and lesson plans? About generativity and leadership along with command-and-control management? And more—how do you have these dialogues in contexts that matter—that are authentic—and that are more than rhetoric at a leadership conference or training session at the beginning of a new year of business or school? How can you be genuine enough to let your fears and learned helplessness begin to fade?

First, you must become consciously aware of your creativity and acknowledge and believe in your heart and mind that you are, in fact, a creative being. You can influence change in yourself and in the world through your voice and actions—*if you choose to do so*. This is about understanding that you are NOT the same as everyone else and that being creative means knowing that you're a little bit weird and unusual. Your balance of the yin and yang, the masculine and feminine sides of being in the world, helps you to get the creative project started, to move it forward and to finish. It helps you see both sides of an issue or design with a wider perspective.

But creativity is not about equality. It's not about being like the men. Creativity is about uniqueness and what YOU bring to the table, about the strength of your intention and your special knowledge and energy. Change and creativity always begin inside you. Your willingness to explore co-creation, living systems and authenticity is part of what makes your journey meaningful. Then, you can begin to develop an awareness of your capacity for creative exploration, technique, structure, and improvisation, and you can take these capacities to the Possibility Space—the unified field where new ideas and actions merge and grow.

How you use your feminine potential matters, as well. Through your determination and commitment, you decide what future state you wish to influence and design. In cooperation with the universe and others in your world, you assess your situation, reflect, learn, invent and take action by using your unique creative voice to make life and work different. You'll be always mindful…always learning… always moving ideas and new products or behaviors into the world. And you'll understand the need to be flexible and filled with the singular integrity that allows you to co-create with the universe.

## CREATIVITY MATTERS

I think we've all learned through the years that creativity means different things to different people. For some, it's relegated to the "high creatives": dancers, choreographers, musicians, artists, architects. To others, a visit to the craft fair at holiday time or in the summer is where they see creativity. Some of us find the gardener, the cook, the glass blower to be the most creative…or perhaps it's the person who lands the deal at the office. Creativity with a "big C" is how many of us have learned to describe those whom we view as more talented than others—who hold the privilege of knowing how to think and behave in more endowed and empowered ways. Creativity with a "little c" is about everyday creativity, what the photographer Dewitt Jones calls the ability to "look at the ordinary and see the extraordinary." (*Everyday Creativity*, 1999) There's no best or perfect way to be creative. There are phases of the process and choices that you'll make to begin, and you'll learn from the suggestions of others about thinking and behaving creatively. (See *Further Reading.*) I'll encourage you to think about building your creativity muscle from the inside-out. But the outcome will depend on your natural capacity to be creative in whatever way you choose.

Creativity matters because it's your natural state of being. You're creative because you *must* be. Period. To not acknowledge your capacity for being openly creative is to be less than authentic and less than an integrated human being. In *The Icarus Deception* (2012), Seth Godin tells us that we know how to be human, and we know how to make art, but sometimes we need permission to do so. His description of "art" makes it clear that we're not artists with a big "C". We're humans "…doing generous work, creating something for the first time, touching another person." (8) I agree. You and I take a look every day and see possibilities that are shining and exciting and meaningful. Acting with this energy can be uncomfortable, especially at work, because most of us have learned to be compliant, to follow directions, to be good girls and good helpers, to avoid risk and certainly to avoid failure—to not use our voices to challenge the status quo. This way of thinking and being in the world is no longer meaningful, nor is it appropriate. Our culture, economic structure, mindsets, and mental models are changing, and all of us need to be courageous enough to not only accept new challenges but also create them. So, grab your big girl clothes—the ones that fit your personality and define who you are—and step up to the magic of using your creative voice. Be original. All that you do is important. You become—then you act. Progress happens. Something new is made. You move it into the world. You finish and begin again. Creativity matters.

## CREATIVE LEADERSHIP MATTERS

Leadership is a choice. Some see themselves as leaders; some don't. Some are okay with being a leader; some aren't. Most of us have learned through the years that leaders are those who can control and influence what other people do. Most likely you've learned that many of them are considered to be the best at their job: the CEO, the scout leader, the orchestra conductor, the coach, the building principal. I've held what have been considered leadership positions throughout my life, beginning, believe it or not, in eighth grade when I was President of Y-Teens at East School in Lancaster, Ohio. During my senior year in high school, I was an officer in four different clubs while studying clarinet at the university, spending long hours in the marching and concert bands, where I sat in "first chair." Then there was the actual time in class and doing homework. And intramural sports. (Not so much here, but I still showed up for basketball and volleyball.) During my senior year in college, I became President of Women's Government—the leadership role for the entire women's student body. It goes on from there. In education there were district roles with arts design and curriculum, administrative roles, state arts organization roles, school board leadership, as well as design and leadership of new programs for teachers and students.

Roles…and more roles…and more roles. This was a great life for a first-born, Type-A personality, and I never much questioned the path. But I have a few questions for you as you consider your creative path—questions that over the years I never asked myself:

☞ *Who is the creative self that lives inside of you?*

☞ *Who is the creative leader that lives inside of you?*

☞ *Where does your creative being begin?*

These are leadership questions that matter. Along with your creative capacity, you have the capability, through the energy that you possess, to influence and lead others by what you say and do, as well as through formal leadership roles. It's like dropping a pebble into the pond: the ripple effect can be enormous. You choose how to use your capacity to observe, listen, talk with others, be mindful and take the chance of being vulnerable while you subtly or assertively move your ideas into the world to be a creative leader. It takes courage and perseverance and a willingness to fail. It happens from the inside-out.

Leadership begins with leading yourself. My friend Leslie Montgomery, a middle school teacher and yoga teacher, says, "If you can lead yourself and change your own thinking, you can help others do the same thing. It starts with us. We need to overcome our fear of being different and accept whatever is inside us that needs to change. This makes us more brave."

Knowing your unique reason for being, how you typically behave in the world, how you make decisions, what's important to you and why, what you really want to accomplish…and knowing that you have possibilities for using your powerful creative voice: all are the beginning. There's no leadership without your intent and your passion. You're the butterfly who speaks—a piece of the puzzle within a larger environment. What you say and do in positive and creative ways will join with the energy directly around you and in the larger universe to gently send energies that influence change in places that you may never imagine and without which the puzzle isn't complete.

I agree with Jean Houston when she tells us that "…too many of the problems in society today stem from leadership that is ill prepared to deal with present complexity." (105) Complexity is our rich, emergent world. We need nimble, flexible, mindful, creative leaders in organizations and schools who influence self-organizing, innovative cultures, and who can help us create order out of chaos. We need leadership for the global, emerging society. This leadership needs to come from a creative woman like you.

## THE CREATIVE LIFE MATTERS

Creativity begins early. Throughout our lives we develop and grow as creative beings. Most of us know by now that children begin to lose the knowledge of their creative capacity once they arrive at school. Our schools and homes are fertile environments for learning as a creative being—or should be. Because of influences in our larger culture and our fears of not competing with other countries and not producing high-achieving young adults, we've seriously erred on the side of standardized testing, state and federal mandates, money as a carrot for accountability, and restrictive evaluation processes that are all in the name of improvement.

We've forgotten to talk about learning. We've forgotten the kids and helping them learn how to build creative lives. As a result, we're losing far too much creative potential in the world. Perhaps you have come through an educational system of "only one right answer" and "the more AP classes the better." Many have. And while we all need to take tests at some time during our lives, learning that this is the only way to measure our achievement and our worth is disabling.

I worked for many, many years with the arts as a teacher, administrator and consultant. I also worked with "integration" of the arts and general education and creative thinking and problem solving with STEM before the current STEAM movement became popular. My experience has shown me that all children of any age learn more deeply, more holistically and more meaningfully through creativity and creative problem solving.

As long ago as the early 1980s, our efforts to evaluate the impact of arts in general education showed that when elementary students involved with a federal Title IV-C grant project learned concepts and skills in mathematics, reading, social studies and science, they scored higher on teacher-designed basic skills tests when they were taught with processes using visual arts, music, dance and drama. Much later, during my tenure as the director of the Macomb Academy of Arts and Sciences in Armada, Michigan, we worked with creative thinking and problem solving as part of scientific research and technology. Our students consistently told us that this, along with the more traditional honors practices in some of their other classes, gave them a great advantage in colleges and universities.

Yet, since the year 2000, educational systems have been systematically reducing the amount of time that our students have to study the arts and experience creativity at all levels. Critical thinking, communication, collaboration and creativity have been labeled 21st Century Skills for all students (The Partnership for 21st Century Skills, or P21). Concepts such as agility, adaptability, initiative, curiosity and imagination appear consistently in the literature and professional development practices for school improvement. This isn't a new movement. It's been around for many years. Unfortunately, too little is done routinely to address our need for creative learning environments in education and to acknowledge the creative capacities that all of our students bring to life and learning. *As a woman, the possibilities for your influence and creative decision making in this segment of our world are endless.* Again, you begin first with you: building your creative life, modeling this life for others, then learning and leading toward a creative life for all around you. Your voice, your being and your leadership matter.

My experiences and opportunities to work with creativity and leadership have been vast. I've been fortunate. All along it seemed that it was something that I *must* do, or, as I like to tell my friends and family, "I cannot *not* do it." It's important to remember that we're all connected. It's about each of us, but it's also about all of us. What I must do and will do impacts you. What you must do and will do impacts me. *We are the system.* We actually create the system and act within the system through our thinking and being individually, as well as co-creating with the universe through our personal and collective energy and will. This is a natural consciousness that we have from birth.

Creativity is a powerful concept. So is creative leadership. We need leaders who can think and behave with sharp minds and open hearts, who can see the world and their work differently, and who can help us co-create in organizations where improvisation and what we believe is "failure" are both a means for learning rather than mistakes that are penalized. We all must be keenly aware, powerfully imaginative and audaciously improvisational.

*In all of the many ways that the creative life is manifest,*
*women will influence.*

Who is the creative self that lives inside of you? Who is the creative leader that lives inside of you? Where does your creative being begin? What *must* you do? What do you *care* about? Creativity reveals, saves and inspires. (Kelly Rae Roberts, 2014) Be aware. Know that what you care about matters. Don't be afraid to be radical.

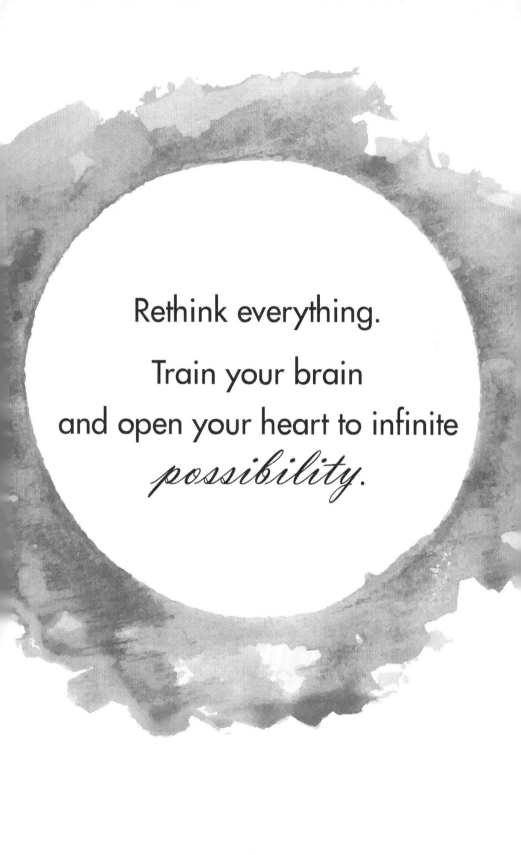

Rethink everything.

Train your brain
and open your heart to infinite
*possibility*.

# CHAPTER 2

# BUILDING YOUR CREATIVITY MUSCLE, PART 1

## *Inside-Out*

# INSIDE ↔ OUT:

IMPROVISATION

CONTEXT

PLAY
*Collaboration*
*Observation*

RISK
*Self-Discovery*
*Flexibility*

POSSIBILITY
SPACE
THE UNIFIED FIELD
NATURAL
EMERGENCE

BOTH/AND
(See-Saw)

PLAN
*Structure*
*Analysis*

# BUILDING YOUR CREATIVITY MUSCLE

## INTUITION

## BE...

### KEENLY AWARE

### POWERFULLY IMAGINATIVE

### AUDACIOUSLY IMPROVISATIONAL

## TECHNIQUE

*Goals*
*Detail*

## PRINCIPLES

*Be original and stand by it.*

*Dance with the dog, and the dog will dance with you.*

*Keep a song in your head.*

## MINDFULNESS

## ACTION

→ *Perform.*

→ *Ship.*

→ *Begin again.*

*There is a vitality, a life force,*
*an energy, a quickening,*
*that is translated through you into action,*
*and because there is*
*only one of you in all time,*
*this expression is unique.*

—Martha Graham

*I*n Western culture we tend to talk about creativity as something separate from us, something that we learn only in an art class or we "own" because someone in our family is talented, and we inherit talent from them. If we have a family, like mine, where music was respected as a part of life, then music can become a natural mode of expression, depending on what we do with it. The same could be true of any art form or creative practice. It becomes part of our experience.

I like to think of creativity as my playground.

Visualize with me an open, inviting playground in a park surrounded by huge oak, pine and maple trees. It's a sun-filled summer day, the air smells clean and sharp, and a slight breeze is blowing. The breeze caresses your face and takes worries and responsibilities away for a bit. Both children and adults are out to enjoy the space and the weather. There's a see-saw, a merry-go-round, swings, a slide, a climbing structure and an old cement water fountain near the parking lot. When you look around, you note that the spacious park is very hilly and green, filled with picnic tables, a smaller shelter house near the playground and a larger, more impressive one built of stone up on the back hill. There's a lovely pond across the drive from the playground and a gazebo near the pond where couples sometimes have weddings, along with park benches around the water where people are sitting watching the ducks. A clay tennis court is a short distance away and is also observable from the playground. If you keep going across the driveway from the pond, you'll find a path to climb "the mountain," a glacier deposit called Mount Pleasant. When you climb to the top of the mountain, you can see most of the city from above and can watch the fireworks at the fairgrounds just across the street on the Fourth of July. Native Americans lived on the mountain in the distant past.

This is a mind's eye view of Rising Park in Lancaster, Ohio, where I spent a memorable time growing up. Even though I didn't want to stay in Lancaster when I left college, I now go there two or three times a year from Michigan and, when I go, I always head to the park to walk, watch people on the playground and sit near the pond. These days, each time I am there I have a positive experience. I feel safe. I remember events in the park throughout my young life, including Camp Fire Girls summer camps, working with handicapped children at day camps where we spent much time at the playground, sunrise services on the mountain on Easter Sunday, family reunions, climbing up the face of the mountain with a friend when I was in eighth grade (not a smart thing to do, but…you know…we were in eighth grade and invincible), playing tennis when I was in college, a last date with my high school sweetheart, and a rehearsal dinner for my first marriage in the large shelter house. Now I experience new perspectives each time I visit. I see with new eyes. I see through many years of experiences and emotions and can go there to find not only quiet and contemplation but also joy and fresh energy.

For now, let's go back to the playground and remember that creativity and creative leadership happen from the inside-out. Our playgrounds can be a meaningful metaphor for what I call Building Your Creativity Muscle. You may be more comfortable visualizing a place that's different from mine. If so, I'm hoping it's a place that's part of you, where you have an emotional attachment to being positive, playful, challenged, and centered, because it seems to me that allowing creativity to be an entity separate from yourself and less than supportive and engaging is damaging. When we don't acknowledge a natural instinct or capacity to play and create, we can never really integrate as a whole living system or be authentic personally and professionally. Creativity, curiosity and improvisation are like muscles: "Use 'em or lose 'em." Building your creativity muscle is ultimately playing full out, running, jumping, spinning, laughing, shouting, feeling free to use your voice—then taking a break and maybe a drink from the old cement water fountain. When you embrace keen awareness, powerful imagination and audacious improvisation, you are free to *be*. It's what happens when nothing is holding you back. (Romanovsky, 2015)

Years ago my friend and colleague Dr. Alexis Lotas and I developed a model that we called "The Teaching Process in the Arts." We worked with artists and teachers who learned together, using a personal development, personality/learning style model while engaging in teaching and the arts process. It worked beautifully for all of us then. The graphic *Inside-Out: Building Your Creativity Muscle* (on p. 42) is an adaptation of this model, albeit much simplified and certainly not at all inclusive. As I go along here, I'll refer to the model occasionally and do my best to use generative language that's the language of creativity, wholeness and expansion while allowing you to see the grounded practice that exists within all learning.

I invite you to use this simple process as a metaphorical playground scenario. Envision the larger context of a playground itself with a merry-go-round in the center, along with other structures, such as a see-saw and a swing—and the principles for growth and expansion are included. Feel free to add other metaphors as you go along. (For example, you may have a climbing structure that becomes an interesting challenge where you'll find new ways to achieve important goals and habits—or you may envision a slide where you move quickly to action. Make the graphic yours.)

*Please remember that creativity is not a linear process and that everything that happens in the playground is interconnected, like a web. As I'll explain, we can only really understand it within the context of the whole.* Rarely, if ever, do we go there and sit only in one place, although we certainly could. Within the energetic field of the playground, everything that happens influences everything else, from movement to voices to relationships to improvisation. This isn't sophisticated or intellectual. I believe you'll see every real playground that you visit differently after exploring our process.

Finally, when you go to your playground, experience the infinite possibilities of your creative being as an unapologetic, strong woman. This will allow you to open to the connection that's your birthright as a vessel for the Divine Feminine, what Andrew Harvey and Anne Baring define as an "...age-old symbol of the invisible dimension of soul and the instinctive intelligence that informs us." (*The Divine Feminine,* 1996, p. 14)

I invite you to participate in creativity and leadership where you can find who you are as a creative being and what you must do creatively in the world through the "invisible flow of energy" that brings ideas, projects, movements, new work constructs and new life into being, "...sustains and transforms it, and withdraws it into a hidden dimension for rebirth and regeneration." (p. 16) These invisible forms of power are rarely, if ever, discussed in our business and school environments, yet they can be felt within your playground and beyond if you are aware and willing to look for them. They demand a connection to what's within you and what you see in the larger landscape. You'll become more open, intuitive, improvisational and mindful, and you'll begin to understand the balance of mind and heart. You'll act with vigor while you design, observe, see both sides, assess, retreat, and begin again, either with something new or a regeneration of your original idea. There are no lists or must do's. You're free to walk through—to *meander* through the scenario (which is itself a feminine capacity)—where you can visualize, experience and choose a place to begin and actions to take. Go again to the graphic, *Inside-Out: Building Your Creativity Muscle.* Here I provide perspectives and practices that have informed me and others, and I'll encourage and push you a bit to find your own creativity playground and to develop capacities that I and others have found to be essential to creative growth and leadership. It will be up to you to decide what you wish to do in the creativity playground and when. As Martha Graham says, there is only one of you in all time. Your expression, as well as your energy, your actions—and your timing— are unique.

## THE CONTEXT: *SCENERY AND SITUATION*

When you focus on being creative, you're training your brain and opening your heart to new ways of thinking and to infinite possibility. You're also committing to allowing your power to influence change. Developing these muscles and the entire structure that supports your creative being allows you to be more open and receptive by developing synapses in the brain and embracing ideas and habits that are part of your personal and professional practice: using "what-if" (divergent) thinking, questioning, imagining, innovating and thinking interdependently. The more you use these capacities, the stronger they grow and the better you become at being creative. Your curiosity, imagination and inspiration, sense of awe, attention and intention and sense of wonder are all engaged when there's an opportunity to be free of undue restrictions and mandates. Because you're unique, each of you will see and hear something slightly different from others, depending on your experience.

I suggest that you begin by exploring the **context** of your playground, either imaginary or real. Develop what my co-authors and I have previously called "situational awareness." (*Generative Leadership*, 2008) Walk around and use your senses for awareness of the situation. Follow the energy. Keep it simple. Be keenly aware of what you see and hear. Who's there? We usually see children and parents or grandparents at a playground. Who's in your playground? Family? Coworkers? Club members? Political committee? Church members? Just you? Who comes to this space to be inspired, play, work and learn? To make a difference? What motivates them? What behaviors do you see? What are they doing? Where are they choosing to play (work)? What are they talking about when they're working? How about when they have breaks and down time? What are the strengths and weaknesses that you observe? (Everyone on the playground is better at something than they are at others.) Are there children and adults who like to participate? To lead? Others who choose to watch? Do you see some who are extroverts and others who are introverts?

Take your time and be patient. Play with this concept for a bit as a beginning practice for your work here. Simply observe and write down what you see in your mind's eye, and if you're ready to do a real observation exercise, choose a playground in real time, go there more than once to see what's up, and make a list or a map or diagram of what's happening in this space. Even though you're keeping it simple, observe carefully and in depth. Watch for relationships and observable energy, and examine your assumptions about what you expect to happen. You'll begin to see stories emerge as you relax and observe.

## BUILDING YOUR CREATIVITY MUSCLE: *INSIDE-OUT*

Now let's transfer our observation and sensing specifically to *Inside-Out: Building Your Creativity Muscle* by beginning with the larger context. I suggest four concepts and practices for your focus: Intuition, Both/And, Mindfulness and Improvisation. You'll find them around the four corners of the playground. These flow throughout your processes of creativity and creative leadership. They're always present and always important to a greater or lesser degree. You'll become more aware of your capacity to listen to your intuition, to be mindful, to see the both/and as well as to respond and act in the moment: that's improvisation. ***Again, none of these four practices happen in a linear manner in your life, they all interconnect and they are all essential to the process. You're free to walk through your life, home, work environment, etc., in any direction that you choose and to walk through from different directions again and again. Each time, begin where it pleases you. You'll find a pattern that works. Then you'll change that pattern if you find it necessary to do so.***

## THE WALK-THROUGHS

# *BEGINNING LOOK-FOR'S AND CAPACITIES*

# INTUITION

Think about the voice inside, inner wisdom, visualizing, being open, receiving, your gut feelings, non-doing, sudden illumination, generativity, energetic knowing.

### *Stop for a moment in this place.*

I want to hear the still, small voice that speaks to me quietly. And from that voice, I want to hear my subtle, inner wisdom. It's that simple. It's about breathing, maybe being where there's no sound but natural sounds around me, visualizing, emptying my "monkey mind," allowing my body to relax, being aware of what's happening with my body. Then there's more breathing, opening, and listening. Sometimes it's about more feeling and less thinking: a felt sense that something must happen or that something isn't right about a situation. Intuition is a natural added dimension that feeds my creativity *and* my creative leadership. It's "…a mysterious, powerful, and subtle ability that every human being possesses and can develop." (Gee, 1999, p. 3)

When I'm out of touch with my intuition, I often find that my overall wellness is compromised, and my creativity is blocked. I find that nature and its rhythms and a quiet mind call my attention to what's not observable. I'm well aware that I'm often too connected to social media, too attached to the TV, too frenzied with worthless talk and meaningless gossip. I'm guessing that many others are, too. Sitting or walking where I can hear my own quiet, intuitive voice that says, "Yes, do this," and "No, don't do that," is critical to my creative life. It's the voice from the universe that holds me to the best energy I know, except the energy that comes with an "Aha!" And it's most often in this receptive, open state that the "Aha!" appears. Your intuition can be heard in many ways and in many places, including your home, your church, walking down the street or taking a shower. Whether you're being creative or not, embrace it. Be sure to pay attention, so that you're aware that your intuition is speaking. Acknowledge your internal creative voice. Don't be afraid or resistant. Try your best to be positive and generative with the universe. The information that you receive here is as important, if not more so, than numerical data. I'm guessing that you might find your creative spirit here, as well.

# MINDFULNESS

Think about awareness, silence, noticing, breathing, listening, attention, clarity, embodiment (physical/emotional), removing the clouds, being in the moment, meditation.

### *Stop for a moment in this place.*

Mindfulness is about being aware of the present moment and paying attention to moment-to-moment changes. It's following your body/mind/soul (spirit) to a new level of awareness. I think of it sort of like being on the swings on the playground, where I can get settled in the swing, push a bit to get going and find a pattern of freedom and focus that helps me feel centered and fresh.

Mindfulness has stepped onto the stage and taken the world by storm recently. Articles, books, and information online about mindfulness in our personal and professional lives are abundantly available. It's part of the creative process, and I think of the practice from two perspectives. First, there is the mindfulness of removing the clouds and seeing the clear blue sky: the silence and inner stillness of meditation, the integration of mind and body, listening to the soul or spirit, the deliberate concentration of energy, walking, being in nature, or sitting quietly on the swing, eyes on a fixed point, and simply being there. There's also the theory and practice of mindfulness in business that's espoused by social psychologist Ellen J. Langer. It includes the concept of "being here now," or "noticing." This is also called "precise observation," which is part of situational awareness, which was mentioned earlier.

I learned this type of mindfulness by walking in the woods when I was younger and noticing the plants, the small shoots of ferns in the spring and early summer, finding moss on the rocks and trees and watching the ducks and geese on the pond. Artists learn early-on to be mindful of specific colors, sounds, movements or words that speak precisely to a message, and classroom teachers use a keen sense of observation and mindfulness every day with students. Both ways of practicing mindfulness are helpful for creativity and creative leadership. I find that the practice of one enhances my capacity to do the other: both/and rather than either/or. When I work with groups on innovation and change, I often challenge them to pay attention, focus and become clear about whatever issue we're exploring; to sharpen their vision and see with new eyes. My question to them is, "What do you notice?" I also give groups time to sit quietly, to focus on the breath, to remove the clouds. These actions fill us with energy and lead to the power of possibility.

Although there are many forms of mindfulness and ways to practice attention, including meditation, yoga, tai chi, qigong, walking and direct exposure to nature, for many practitioners the sitting practice of *mindful meditation* has been the place to begin. What I look for in my sitting practice, which is never perfect and always evolving, could be called emptiness and being centered. If I can focus, even for a moment or two, on my breath, allow the monkey mind to float in and out (mine rarely goes away entirely), and practice letting go and being empty and clear, what comes for me is openness, a connection to my intuition and the capacity to focus. You don't need to learn how to fabricate creativity. You can learn to mindfully follow your creative being to the Possibility Space and to a new world of experience. Learning to focus your attention so that your best being and work can emerge is well worth the effort.

# BOTH/AND

Think about balance, the center, the fulcrum, rational/emotional, mind/heart, masculine/feminine, think/feel, from/to, yin/yang.

Take a minute and wander over to the see-saw (teeter-totter).

### *Stop for a moment in this place.*

I used to love the see-saw at the park and at the elementary school when I was young. We had what I like to think of as *real* see-saws: the ones that were hefty, made of wood, heavy and substantial. They were gutsy. No plastic, safe ones for us. I learned to play on them in first grade. (We didn't have kindergarten when I was young, and I didn't play in the park much then.) When I was on the see-saw with a friend, we thought the pushing up and going down was a test to see how fast we could go to make our stomachs go up into our throats. We had to push, and we had to sense where the lift/drop could be. We hoped beyond hope that our friend didn't jump off and let us crash to the ground, so we were always a bit on guard to be able to catch ourselves if this happened. We were really watchful, no matter what. I also used to stand in the center of the see-saw alone, one foot on each side of the fulcrum, and try to balance the plank as well as possible. It was necessary to shift a bit from side to side to make this happen. (I don't remember doing this much in first grade, but by the time I was in fourth or fifth, I could handle it.)

The see-saw is about perspective and energy, and, like mindfulness, there are two ways that I think of it as a metaphor for our dialogue about creativity and leadership. First, there is the two-player give and take of going from one side to the other, with the relationship of the players keeping the focus on movement. There is significance to knowing that there are differences on each end, and that the differences are real and important. For example, you'll want to be intense and analytical when necessary, but softer and more intuitive at other times. (Wilson, *Finding the Quiet*, 2009) Each side must work together to make the see-saw move effectively. Secondly, when I stand in the center, the see-saw provides a *balance* of two concepts: familiar/unknown, rational/emotional, formal/informal, yin/yang, inside/outside, masculine/feminine. The easiest way for me to think of it is this: On one side is the question, "What do I think?" On the other side, the question is, "What do I feel?" Sometimes I can get there with "What is linear?" and "What is non-linear?" On one side are the rigor, technique, formal structures, analysis, theory—"How do I move this forward?"—that require active, overt, masculine energy:

intense and analytical. On the other are curiosity, inspiration, emotion, openness, the unknown. "What must I hear and feel to be creative?" On this side is subtle, nurturing, feminine energy: softer and more intuitive. You can play with the both/and in a variety of ways and use any terminology that you wish.

In our book, *Generative Leadership: Shaping New Futures for Today's Schools* we talk about the both/and as a "from-to" strategy, which may be a more familiar concept for you. (We knew that the perceptions and behaviors would go both ways. You would go back and forth between the old and new ways of thinking.) No matter how you decide to play with the see-saw, there's no limit to finding an abundance of ideas on either side, and it dismisses a black and white perspective. It's what you'll come to know as the "creative tension" that exists in life and in leadership, what John Kao in *Jamming* (1996) calls "certain vital human tensions, or paradoxes." (32)

Sometimes one side of the see-saw is up and the other down. You'll stay up or down depending on where you want to be with issues and your planning and creative process. There seems to be no right or wrong, and there's no failure as we know it: only consideration for one or both sides. One of our current problems in schools and organizations is that we spend an inordinate amount of time on one side of the see-saw, with structure and linear thinking that get their hold on us. We don't let them go, more often than not because we're afraid of what might happen (the unknown) if we do, and because we've been taught to think and be in control this way. It's as if the fulcrum has moved closer to one end, leaving the other as longer and heavier and impossible to balance. In our culture and in our attempts to control change and productivity, we've been so concerned about the bottom line, mandates, testing and evaluating and structures that define our work and life, that we get stuck there and wonder why we can't come up with something different. You can go the opposite way as well, of course, with the fulcrum off-center again, and spend so much time receiving and being reflective and open that you never take rigorous action to finish a project or produce something meaningful, if you produce anything at all. Right now, in this moment, you're transitioning from your old energy platforms, your mental and energetic models, and you need to rethink everything—to balance from the center, even for a short time, and to acknowledge that your voice is critical to this balance. You cannot move forward effectively without knowing how to balance your masculine and feminine psyche, the analytical and emotional body/mind/soul, so that you can create holistically and co-create with friends and colleagues who play and learn and plan with you and support your efforts. In your personal and professional lives you'll need to look at both sides to find what makes you whole. And at some point you'll want to find the sweet spot where the magic happens—in the center—then stay there for as long as you can before you begin to go up and down again. This requires mindfulness and reflection, slowing down and paying attention—the opposite of simply reacting.

My friend Stacey King, a high school math teacher and former choreographer, has a problem with the words "creative" and "leader." "I hate that word *creative*," she says. "It's like the word *leader*. I'm not sure what either of them really means in my world. I like to dot the i's and cross the t's." Stacey sees herself as sitting mostly on one side of the see-saw, and she's fairly open about how she's learned to see the world. Yet, she teaches in one of the most creative programs in Michigan, used to love to choreograph, and I've known her to always look for the both/and. Her teaching is full of creative ideas and problems for her high school algebra students. She surrounds herself with colleagues who consistently push her to use her creativity. Perhaps she sees them on the other side of her see-saw. The fact that she's immersed in both dialogue and practice that require creativity from the group—and herself—is significant. This environment allows her to co-create in ways that not only require her "dotting i's and crossing t's" but also allow her to play, improvise, and look for possibilities. Some of us can stand in the center of the see-saw and balance on our own. Others like partners to help them play. You'll benefit from experiencing both. Stacey chooses to see the discipline of math and play with art, and she contributes and learns in meaningful and exciting ways.

# IMPROVISATION

Think about play, creation, the unknown, focus, being in the moment, discovery, being open, ambiguity, saying "Yes" vs "No," change, being co-creative, everyday life, being generative, being active, and possibility.

### *Stop for a moment in this place.*

Improvisation holds the spirit of creativity, and it means creating in the moment without a plan. More often than not, it's playful. It's the ultimate act of welcoming the unknown. Robert Lowe, in *Improvisation, Inc.* (2000), offers a definition of improvisation as making "…use of the tools and resources at hand without reference to expected results; to improvise, to deal in the unforeseen, to take part in the act of creation." (12). My friend and colleague Stephanie DeMarco, a biochemist who teaches middle school science and high school dance, says improvisation is trying something you've never seen or done before, [then] responding and learning from it. And Elaine Bezas, a lawyer friend in our county, believes that improvisation is very important. Lawyers have no idea what the judge is going to say. She always anticipates that she may need a response or plan that might not have been expected—to be able to play with what's happening in the moment.

Improvisation means that you let go of preconceived ideas about control, pay attention to your intuition as well as other people if you're interacting, be willing to be vulnerable and to challenge your capacity for creativity in open and positive ways. It requires imagination and being prepared for the unexpected. Saying "Yes" rather than "No" opens the space for positivity and possibility, which can greatly influence your work. It can happen both in co-creative groups and on an individual level during small minutes and longer hours of each day, and it helps to sit on the open, inspirational side of the see-saw and be willing to challenge the status quo. Improvisation takes focus, attention, a willingness to go into a "discomfort zone," and, if you've never done this as a practice, where a high level of awareness and intention are required, you'll most likely feel really, really uncomfortable at first. Your life is improvised much more than most realize, and your struggle to control every minute—or the organization's mandate to control every minute—is the antithesis of improvisational thinking and behavior.

Improvisation is embedded in activity and is generative: one thought or action can spontaneously lead to another. Those who do improvisational theater, dance or music, especially jazz, are hyper-alert to what's happening around them and to their choice of a response. They forget about the script or the choreography or the sheet music and create in the moment. It's forgetting about the word or the step or the note you just played and moving immediately to the new one, and it demands relaxing into the moment and allowing new ideas and actions to come through. Improvising means that you'll need to let go. You'll need to be able to laugh at yourself and find joy in the beauty of the moment—to be spontaneous— and also to step back and allow others to take the lead. I like to think of improvisation (as well as generativity) as thousands of small moments during the day when I step into the center of the merry-go-round, into the Possibility Space, and step out with something different to just "allow"—not fear, judge or become cynical about my capacity for a creative life. For me, that's how it begins. Just *allow*.

I also like to "erase." When a process wasn't going well in my classroom years ago and if it currently isn't working during facilitation sessions with adults, I often will laugh and say to the students or participants, "Let's just stop and erase that. We'll start again." Improvisation is about play, teamwork, focus and flexibility. It's about letting go and paying attention.

Be different.

Be courageous.

It's about
emergence,
openness,
reflection,
discovery,
courage,
and *sustenance*.

# CHAPTER 3

# BUILDING YOUR CREATIVITY MUSCLE, PART 2

## *The Possibility Space*

*It is from our collective powers of creativity
that the most important
human achievements have flowed...*

—Ken Robinson,
*Finding Your Element*

*S*o, here we are, still in the park and on the playground, and now it's time to take a breath and skip over to the merry-go-round, where our focus will be on your important preferences for beginning the creative process. Just as Intuition, Mindfulness, the See-Saw and Improvisation are always around in the park, the Merry-go-round will always be there for your pleasure and your work. In a playground, a merry-go-round is usually a simple, child-powered rotating platform with bars or handles that children can cling to when they're riding. (I'm not thinking of the carousel with horses—which is one of my favorite rides at the fair.) On the playground, this is a structure within the larger field. In the graphic *Inside-Out: Building Your Creativity Muscle* (p. 42), I've given you four seats along with the larger center that holds, balances and gives sustenance, if you will, to the structure. The center is of primary importance, since we couldn't ride the merry-go-round without it. For our metaphor, I'll begin there.

## IN THE CENTER: *THE POSSIBILITY SPACE*

The center of the merry-go-round is an anchor for experiencing the creative process. It's the core of the structure that allows it to move once the periphery is elevated. Most of us don't stand there when we ride, but on merry-go-rounds that are built to allow us to move to the center, we're free to go there when we want to slow down, reflect and just ride along. We can also see the seats from a very different perspective. There are four seats surrounding the center, each holding a place for entering the merry-go-round. It looks as if there's a space for standing between the seats, as well. Having the connections from each seat to the center means that you can move back and forth at will, and you can stand between them. The center is our Possibility Space.

I like to think of the Possibility Space—sometimes called the white space, the blank page, or a clean-sheet design perspective—as an energy field for imagination, excitement, reflection, silence, and exploration. Sometimes the space is tangible, like the center of the merry-go-round, where it's quieter and feels slower, the painter's canvas, the composer's score sheet, the dancer's white room, the planning map, or the proverbial blank page for the writer. Sometimes it's virtual and lives in our minds or hearts—or is invisible within dialogue at the organizational table. It's always a generative space, and at its foundation it really is a psychic space. Clarissa Pincola Estés speaks of the archetypal lore where "...there is the idea that if one prepares a special psychic place, the being, the creative force, the soul source will hear of it, sense its way to it, and inhabit that space." (Estés, 1992, p. 299)

Some artists refer to this as the Muse. Here is where new ideas, new forms and possibility reside and emerge. Some will see and feel this energy as a force to impel you to create. Others will be aware of the unified field of interconnection within the universe. This will all depend on the level of your awareness of emergence and complexity around you and of your creative voice inside, along with your willingness and desire to make something new and different. You won't always be able to predict which seat you'll take on the merry-go-round at any given moment, or how fast it will go, or who else will be there, but it's here in the center where all of the processes for creativity are unified if you wish to acknowledge its power. It's really a resting, meditative place within the structure. Many of us welcome this natural space, and we all fear it to some extent. At the very least, it's impossible to ignore.

You may choose to actually go to the park and stand in the center of the merry-go-round. You may have different favorite places to consider possibility. But, no matter where you are working or writing or thinking, if you forget to enter the psychic space where the soul of your thinking and passion reside, the physical space will be negligible. It's about emergence, openness, reflection, discovery, courage and sustenance. All are invisible at first, and all are powerful.

## CHOOSE A SEAT: *FOUR ESSENTIALS TO DEVELOP YOUR CREATIVITY MUSCLE*

You can choose to sit anywhere on the merry-go-round, but most likely you'll favor some seats (or spaces) over others. Your tendency will be to go where you're most comfortable, even though the seats may seem identical at first. If you're mindful and notice specifics, there'll be slight differences. One may have some paint missing, another may have a scratch or be just slightly higher. On our metaphorical merry-go-round, each seat will have different behaviors, a different focus and a different voice. All four are important, so you'll want to be sure to know what can happen there and move around from seat to seat. Remember that there'll be both women and men on the merry-go-round, and your voice may change depending on the context. For this practice, find your seat and hold your seat for a while (pay attention to how your body/mind feels there). As you get better at moving from one seat to another, you'll begin to notice your internal voice—your voice of creativity. You'll know when it's important to move into the Possibility Space then out again.

# THE PLAY SEAT

When you jump on the Play Seat, you'll be attracted to playing, collaborating and visualizing. More often than not, you're a people-person, and you prefer working with others, perhaps in pairs or small groups. I've learned to sit in all four seats, and have found this one is quite comfortable for me. I'm an extrovert who is very social, and I need to share what I'm creating and get feedback and ideas from friends and colleagues. I usually do this early and easily. If I were an introvert, I might spend more time reflecting privately about what I observe before sharing, if I like to share at all. In the play seat, you're what I affectionately call a "putzer." You like playing with forms and ideas, day dreaming, exploring, and fantasizing. You connect easily with your intuition and pay attention to emotions. You'll spend time observing, sensing and nurturing the context and the relationships that develop around you. This is one of the wonderful messy spots where you can play and not really be required to produce—just yet. The downside of this seat is that you can play here forever and never really finish a project or take your work out to a greater community.

## PLAY AND THE CREATIVE PROCESS

There is always a phase of the creative process where play is necessary. Actually, we play throughout, but in this seat it becomes our focus. If you like trying out new recipes (even if they fail); working with new materials with painting, constructing, gardening; trying out new ideas at the office; mind-mapping to explore; or picking up a drum and just banging on it for the fun of it, play is at the center. Both my father and my mother liked this type of activity. Daddy played in the vegetable garden and taught himself to play the guitar. Mother liked sewing and creating new dresses for her three daughters, and she was a crafter who created pine cone wreaths from scratch without a pattern. My parents grew up in a time when people didn't take lessons to learn; they learned from someone in the family, began on their own or maybe joined a club where everyone was learning something new. Sometimes there was a childlike joy and fun to their work. Other times it was simply the way they lived and worked or, in the case of the garden and sewing, it provided food and clothes for the family. If you teach or are a parent or grandparent, watch your children play without supervision. Sense the quality of their focus, deliberation, exploration and dialogue. That's the spirit of this seat on the merry-go-round.

## ENERGY AND INTENTION/THE HABIT OF PLAY

Begin developing this part of your creative muscle by slowing down, using all of your senses to perceive a process or problem and letting go of the mindset of being perfect from the start. Look for inspiration. What do you see? How do you want to experiment? Do you have an idea? What does it look like, sound like, smell like, feel like, taste like? Write this down with great detail in your journal. Allow yourself to be open enough to play with your new concept in a way that may feel different. Don't worry if it doesn't seem rational. Actually, that's the point. Take time to look…and look again…and look again. Slow down and be mindful of how creative you feel in this seat. *What does your creative voice tell you?* My friend Suzanne Culver, whom you'll meet later in this book, reminds me that "We choose to live in such a crazy fashion. We need to learn to get quiet and let things happen. There's real freedom in that." Follow this energy and allow yourself to begin to simply explore and use your senses to see what emerges. Share what you're learning when you're ready.

# THE TECHNIQUE SEAT

I'm an oldest child and a Type A personality who learned very early to be a classical musician. This is the seat that I used to believe was the best place to begin. I've learned to be more adaptive, but this was where I could learn the skills, set goals for performance, pay attention to details. It's the rationale for first concentrating on "what" and "how" before exploring "possible." The Technique Seat is a necessary part of the creative process and certainly of creative leadership—training the mind and the hands—to think and practice, following the rules. If you are someone who prefers to sit here, you will love drill and memorization, along with structured experiences for creating, either alone or with others. In my workshops, teachers and administrators who prefer this seat or who believe that it comes first, will often say to me, "Just tell me what to do." Once they know *what* to do and *how* to do it, moving forward to create something new is easier. This fits on the managerial/technical side of the see-saw, for instance, where detail and management are a focus. When you're working with creativity and leadership, it's wise to remember that you can't ignore this seat and that you can't create something of value or improvise from nothing. It takes technique to be excellent, no matter how you learn it.

However, in our culture and our schools, this seat is malfunctioning, and it's often broken. Too many of you, your colleagues and your children are struggling to sit here way too long even when you're uncomfortable and not learning. You'll need to sit in this seat *for a while*, and of course you'll always need to come back to keep your technique sharp and accurate—to ongoing training. It's difficult to read, for example, if you don't know how to decipher words, sentences and phrases or understand what the words mean…but choose to jump off and shift to another seat when you must. I knew many musicians who could sit in the practice room for hours—much longer than I would—but eventually, once they learned the music and the technique, they needed to play somewhere other than all alone in a room where no one heard them. You'll want to do something with the technique that you possess.

All of the seats are important. You'll need to experience the perspective and feeling of sitting in all of them. Remember that this is YOUR creative voice. You can stay in the technique seat as long as you like and be very comfortable. You can also jump off and try another and then return. Listen to your creative voice. It's your choice.

## TECHNIQUE AND THE CREATIVE PROCESS

When I want to learn technique, I take a class or use a manual. It can be for music, tai chi, writing, whatever. I need to practice, to train my mind and my body to work correctly with the form or domain, and I need to get better at it over time. Here is where "use it or lose it" is obvious. For example, expert photographers take hundreds of photographs to choose only one or two for publication or competition. Creative leaders spend time learning how to organize dialogues, be good listeners, know the principles of effective leadership and improvise. They get feedback along the way, double-check their practices and accept the fact that what seems like failure is really an opportunity to move to the next level of learning. They go to workshops and classes to learn. In a complex system, you have many opportunities to disrupt the status quo and make new constructs for living, working and learning. You'll need to sense and analyze what to do and then know how to do it well. Train your technique. But don't forget that there are other seats on the merry-go-round that are equally important.

## ENERGY AND INTENTION/HABITS FOR TECHNIQUE

Find a good teacher and practice, practice, practice. If you're learning on your own, practice, practice, practice. Create a disciplined structure for strengthening this creative muscle. Focus on detail. How do you want to create? What skills do you have that are natural for this creative endeavor, idea or leadership role? What skills and capacities do you need to learn and develop? How much effort are you willing to give? Who will teach you? Where will you go to immerse in new techniques? How strongly do you feel about learning new things? *What does your creative voice tell you?*

## THE PLAN SEAT

Ahhhh. Here's the seat that I struggle with again and again. This is my weakest seat. But debaters will sit in this seat until the cows come home, and that's a long time if no one goes to get them. Those who love to analyze data or create an argument and rebuttal, who love structure and form, who appreciate the correct posture of ballet, yoga, and sitting up correctly to play a musical instrument thrive in this seat. I have many friends who are debaters and musicians, and they sit here periodically, sometimes "til the cows come home." My son is a web designer and, as you know, a photographer. I've seen him begin from this "shaped" perspective. Those who prefer to begin here seem most comfortable with knowing that there's a map or a pattern that holds them securely before jumping out to create, and designing and creating structures is often their project of choice. Students in this seat are comfortable with research projects, inquiry, independent learning and projects that allow them to use their thinking and intuition. Think of standing up and feeling the center of your body and focusing on the diaphragm, as if you were doing ballet. Now stand on one leg. Shape your body to hold your balance. Because there is a physical center for each of the seats as well as a mental/emotional preference, if this is easy for you, you'll most likely love the plan seat.

## PLAN AND THE CREATIVE PROCESS

I'll push you as we go along to be more open, receptive and improvisational as a creative being. If you like planning, analyzing and structure, you may find these behaviors and the Possibility Space quite uncomfortable at first. You might ask, "What's expected of me here, and why am I here, for Pete's sake? What am I supposed to do? How come this space feels so open and scary?"

These are real issues for women who grew up with form and structure as safety nets, so don't be surprised if you find yourself questioning and analyzing the real purpose of any or all parts of the creative process. In a complex adaptive system, form and structure are important. They're what help us see the real picture and define reality. Developing the capacity to change and simply knowing that you will feel lost and vulnerable for a time is also critical. I have a friend who loves to be spontaneous when she's traveling. She likes to explore unknown territory. However, I've seen that same friend get lost more than once because she didn't have a map or didn't know where the road might go when it was getting dark. She panicked. Literally. It's an interesting paradox. I know others who have been in leadership sessions with me or who have been members of my staff at the academy who have difficulty when there's a break from the typical school routine. We all have safety zones and configurations where we feel most comfortable. Like Technique…this seat is essential to developing your creative muscle. Take the time to design the shape of your idea and creative work.

Again, when you begin here, be sure to jump off the merry-go-round and try another seat, especially when you're developing your muscle as an individual. If you're working with a team, share your preferences for structure authentically and invite others to do the same with their styles. Learn from each other and capitalize on everyone's strength. The merry-go-round gets stuck and doesn't move if no one is willing to be adaptive. Give yourself time to plan and organize your thoughts—to be focused, to see with clarity, to see the big picture. Then take a big breath and explore.

## ENERGY AND INTENTION/HABITS FOR PLAN

In my earlier book, *Generative Leadership/Shaping New Futures for Today's Schools,* we offered various tools that creative leaders could use for planning and dialogue. We knew that some leaders wouldn't need these tools; others would be lost without them. Some will like a graph or chart to organize the development of their creative muscle. Others like to work in a more free-form environment. In the Plan seat, visual planning forms, a good matrix, charts, lists and pyramids are significant. You may want to use your own or go to those you've found from others. If the visual or strategic plan is what gives you a foundation for creative license to think more expansively or allows you to be more generative, then the habit of finding these and having them on hand for planning and dialogue is certainly advisable. However, your imagination and ingenuity will be the key ingredients for creative thinking and behavior. What do you want to do? How do you imagine your plan or structure developing? What inspires you to examine and analyze with a critical, discriminating eye? How much time do you need to organize your thoughts and designs? What questions do you need to ask? How are you willing to be innovative? *What does your creative voice tell you?*

# THE RISK SEAT

Later in this book, I'll ask you to be original and stand by it. I'll be asking you to be a divergent thinker: to be open, free, intuitive, consider possibilities, stand in the center of the see-saw, play on the swings and the climbing structure, then go sit and be mindful for a bit. In the Risk seat you'll be eager to do some self-discovery and to be a flexible thinker, and more often than not improvisation will be very comfortable for you. This seat is a blessing for many but a continued threat to others who are working so hard to develop their creativity muscle. Taking risks means that you can sit anywhere and move freely throughout the playground, and it means that you use your creative voice without too much concern about negative responses. I believe our schools are where this particular opportunity to awaken your creative voice is least encouraged. Consequently, we learn to fear the possibility of being scorned for original thoughts, being creative, and being different or being "wrong."

As I write this, my granddaughter Maebel is two years old. What delights me most about watching her play is the freedom and joy that she seems to feel when she's doing something fun or learning something new. She can go from jumping through the room while she sings a song to focusing intently on drawing with markers on a huge sheet of paper or building with blocks. She'll be flexible, eager, sometimes funny and demanding...then she falls asleep. She'll scrunch up her face in disgust when there's food on her hands but will play in the barn stall with the potbellied pigs with not a care in the world. You may not be able to function as Maebel does on a daily basis, but it's important to find your way to the Risk seat so that you can experience freedom and self-discovery. If this is where you prefer to begin, be as authentic in the world as you can and don't apologize for sitting here. If you're experimenting with this seat, I'm pleased for you. Be as self-aware, spontaneous and adaptive as you can. Take a huge breath, look around and see with new eyes.

## RISK AND THE CREATIVE PROCESS

If you're looking for a place to practice risk quickly and easily, I suggest you begin with improvisation: the sweet spot in the center of the see-saw and the tension between reading the sheet music and free play. Be like John Coltrane, famed jazz saxophone player and composer, who plays by starting in the middle of the sentence and going in both directions at once. You'll not be able to create with just one side or the other. It's not either/or. Improvisation is a way of life.

All of your conversations are improvisational in nature. You begin talking with another person, paying attention to what they're saying. You respond, listen, respond again, all in the present moment. You never know what will come of any dialogue that you engage in or initiate. You take the risk of not being understood, of not understanding and of saying something that you don't mean. Taking a risk means having a strong will to make something new that's of value—something that matters. Let yourself go and flow through the process as if there is nothing holding you back, just as you do when you're in an animated dialogue with another person or a group at work. Be willing to respond in the moment with what comes from your mind and heart, to show your ideas without fear. This is more than hard to do, I know. For some it will take practice, and you're certainly allowed to practice quietly and alone until you find a way to share.

Here is an affirmation that I've used for many, many years:

*"I am a positive, proactive, creative and courageous woman."*
*(…leader, artist, musician, whatever)*

I began writing down this affirmation when I was in my forties and was ready to make a career change. If you checked my journals from that time until now, you'd find the affirmation there. It works this way: When it's time to take risks, it's important that I know who I am. This is who I'd like to be. Always. And I think it's worked pretty well over the years. You'll find your way to self-discovery and creativity by believing that it's possible to go there. That's the first step. If you need this type of affirmation first, be sure to sit in the Risk seat at the very beginning. Stay there…be uncomfortable…then get comfortable. Create from what moves you. *Listen to your creative voice.* Improvise, stop, try again, breathe. Make something new or improve something and make it better. Then be willing to take another risk, and try the other three seats on the merry-go-round.

## ENERGY AND INTENTION/HABITS FOR RISK

Are you a generative being? Can you rethink, reframe, remake? Can you create a final piece that's ready to go out in the world? Are you willing to be messy? To find your true creative expression? Your true reason for leadership? Can you accept the value of daydreaming and being contemplative? Are you willing to be open and flexible? Developing habits for Risk means you must let go or be shoved. The field of infinite possibility is always more available when you're authentic. If you want to experience your creativity, then you must allow your creative being to come forward with freedom, joy and a good shout of your authentic, creative voice, and you must be ready to implement your fledgling idea. Be willing to rethink everything, to be fearless, curious and filled with wonder. Color outside the lines. Think and write in metaphors. Be positive about your new skills and ideas. Be an artist in whatever way suits you, at home and at work. Be different.

## PAY ATTENTION TO YOUR AUTHENTIC VOICE: *BE UNIQUE*

On the merry-go-round, you may decide to go to the Possibility Space alone, or someone else might move into the space with you. You can play on the playground alone, but more often than not, lots of others are there to play at the same time. The metaphor works well for you as an individual woman who might like to be more creative and use the graphic for *Inside-Out: Building Your Creativity Muscle* (p. 42) as a springboard for journaling, goal setting or contemplation.

When you take the playground concept to work as a creative leader, you'll not be alone. Your context will be different, and you'll use the suggestions from a larger perspective of influence. Both are necessary, and the see-saw later will help you find a balance. It's just fine to stay in the center of the merry-go-round for a while, then leave to meander through the park when you feel the need and the desire to explore and find the larger perspective: for example, to sit on the swing and be mindful, to walk quietly and listen to your intuition, to improvise with a design or idea. None of these will feel as if they're separate from the other. I break them down into parts for you, so that you can see each as an important element of the creative system, but they are all in relationship. In a complex adaptive system all of the behaviors and choices are holistic and organic, and there's a flow where they all influence each other.

Once you've tried the seats on the merry-go-round and have walked a bit around the park, pay attention to the energy for moving your creative being and ideas into the world. Along with context intelligence or situational awareness, listening to your intuition, being mindful, playing on the see-saw and improvising, you'll want to bring something new into your world. Ultimately, you'll want to perform or ship your work, or whatever, and *begin again*. You'll want to act with courage and intent and strong will—to sit on the masculine side of the see-saw. This rich flash of energy begins with knowledge of yourself, your personal voice and your willingness to use your influence to make something different. What do you want and how do you show up? Are you an introvert—a subtle energy person, or an extrovert—a more outwardly assertive, visibly energetic person? Are you a rose that needs consistent care and nurturing or a daisy that is eager to spread your wings, grow wild and color the landscape with your freedom?

The world today begs for subtle energy that moves toward action. Know your style and where you prefer to begin within the creativity-muscle spectrum: 1) sensing and playing with ideas or materials through trial and error, 2) learning the technique or practical application, 3) understanding the structure of processes through concepts or models, or 4) improvising and being imaginative with a small part of the larger project before you begin designing. Check your assumptions about your context and about the styles of others around you—in your personal and professional life. Encourage those around you to do the same. As trite as it still may sound, creativity and creative leadership begin with you, no matter what your position of influence. Your energy is contagious, and you'll be vulnerable. Pay attention to your context and know how the system around you is working. Learn when and how to use your creative voice most effectively. You'll build the resilience and self-confidence to be the best that you can be. Surround yourself with friends and colleagues. Your collective energy and spirit will open doors for powerful imagination. Then finish your work and send it out. Begin again. There is only one unique you. It's your time, and we need you. Be a courageous woman.

You are creativity
and possibility.

You're at the center of the
*design.*

# CHAPTER 4

# LIVING IN THE POSSIBILITY SPACE

## *Body, Mind and Soul*

*Orville Wright did not have
a pilot's license.*

—Gordon MacKenzie,
*Orbiting the Giant Hairball*

*W*hen you live in the Possibility Space, you choose to enter with your body, mind and soul. It's your psychic space, where your soul resides, and it's a powerful energetic force for your creativity. Own that space. It's a source of intuitive information and sustenance for your being. Slow down, get quiet, breathe, and be mindful of your authentic inner voice—your voice of creativity. If you're working with the merry-go-round, you might want to visualize the structure stopping its movement and being still, as if there were no one but you on the playground, where the breeze is soft and quiet. Then you can enter the unlimited, unified field of energy where you'll find synchronicity, felt meaning, and discovery that emerges naturally through you and expands throughout the field of the playground and beyond. Out there, when you're ready, you'll begin to co-create with others and with the universe. Once you step over to the energy flash of performing, shipping and beginning again, you must be ready and willing. You must move quickly without too much thought or questioning and be aware that the idea you have may not be just right. But first, there are the possibilities.

Dancer, choreographer and author Twyla Tharp describes the white room that's her studio in downtown Manhattan, where she often begins her choreography. It's surrounded by eight foot high mirrors with a boom box in the corner and nothing on the floor but scuff marks. (Tharp, 2003) It's just Twyla and the room: her Possibility Space. Stepping into that space gives her the opportunity to create something new, reflect on work that's already been done, combine the two, or leave with nothing to share but a great deal to consider for future work. She works with the whole of the system that is the dance, even as she isolates individual sections, steps and ideas. There's connection to play, technique, planning and risk taking. It all takes courage and not a small amount of persistence. She may simply leave with just a spark of an idea, but the idea surrounds all of her: body, mind and soul.

## RESISTANCE VS SAYING "YES!"

I was a dancer for a short time in my life and found that stepping into any large space that's full of potential for the body, mind and soul working together can be exhilarating—if you're ready to listen to yourself, use your technique, explore, learn and create. Your Possibility Space doesn't need to be as large and open or have eight-foot-high mirrors (scary thought) as Twyla Tharp's studio. We're thinking of it as the center of a merry-go-round, after all. Here's another image. Try imagining the Possibility Space as sort of an organic shape that's drawn on the floor near your desk or chair. You could actually draw one on a large sheet of paper if that works for you or find a colorful piece of cloth that you can put on the floor and "step into." Visualize standing and actually stepping into that space—or take a break from reading this book and actually stand up and move to a different spot. Think of this as your Possibility Space. You'll feel a bit silly, but that's what happens when you begin to open up and think differently. How does anticipation of standing in that space feel emotionally…physically…mentally? Imagine the energy of positive change and your innate power for creativity moving from the earth through your feet, into your body and up your spine to above your head. Allow yourself to relax, even for a few minutes, with the whole of you being in a space of emptiness and readiness. This can be the beginning of *allowing* when you enter the Possibility Space. Being open and receptive, alone or with others, is important. Remember, awareness matters. Pay attention to what happens with your body and how you feel physically. Now focus on how you feel emotionally. And then write about what you're feeling and thinking. Be sure to note anything that's even a tiny bit new and different for you. There are no right answers here. Simply be aware.

Because the Possibility Space holds the unknown, living there even for a short time can be frightening if you want a plan or first want to learn a technique. Those who fear the space might downshift temporarily, feel anxious or have a difficult time breathing—it's fight/flight/freeze. We've known for many years that it is a myth that emotions, learning, creativity and physical activity, or taking action on an idea, are separate. You are a holistic living system. You react and respond from that state of being. Consequently, if you fear the Possibility Space, you can feel weak and out of balance. You stop thinking.

Alternatively, you may find comfort in the Possibility Space but fear stepping outside. You can actually step in and stand there indefinitely, liking the feeling of almost-creating, but then be afraid to go back or to step out the other side, knowing for sure that your ideas won't work or will be ridiculed or dismissed. Many women in the work force repeatedly experience this fear. If this is true for you, the Possibility Space can become a dark cave. Because most of us have learned to hide in dark caves, you stand and stand and sit and stand and lie down and get up to stand again but mostly just exist there and then get out as quickly as possible. We all commit to our comfort zone, and on most days hiding in the cave where it's safe is more important for us than exploring or being generative. You convince yourself that you're doing what's right by being there and that the longer you reflect the better your ideas will be. It's a place where, if you allow it, your voice becomes still and silent with resistance for all the wrong reasons, even though those reasons are so real at the time. You live in a creative world, and, like Orville Wright, you don't always have a pilot's license. Knowing why you fear the space, how you resist it, how you can prepare your mind and emotions and body to be ready to create is part of your individual and collective work, both at home and at work. If you wish to become a creative leader, it's imperative that you be aware that resistance is "…an energy field radiating from a work-in-potential. It's a repelling force. Its aim is to shove us away, distract us, prevent us from doing our work." (Pressfield, 2002, p. 97) Staying in the Possibility Space as long as you need to and stepping out with positivity and courage to be proactive is a rite of passage for creative leaders.

If you welcome the challenge of the unknown, of exploration and the possibility of something new and exciting, the Possibility Space is made to order. It's a part of your reality and your daily experience. You say "Yes!" to living there. You learn to listen to your intuition, to allow your soul—the authentic you—to speak and feel as well as think about what you're about to do. You think of it as a space that can take you somewhere, and when you're ready, you commit to action, step out and move quickly and decisively. Stepping into a big space—maybe the entire playground when no one else is there—can be daunting, even though at some point it's necessary, but going there with others is what we sometimes call brainstorming, clean-sheet designing, or group improvisation. All of these can be learned, and once you find that you're able to move through the fear that your ideas or actions will be dismissed or ignored, being there is more than empowering. You like the challenge of creating from the blank page. You learn to become less afraid over time. You feel the rich energy of forward movement toward a new idea. At the very least, you learn to recognize and know resistance and how to move through a very natural reaction to starting something new. You ask questions: "Why am I here?" "What matters in this space?" "What do I want to design/ create?" "Who else needs to be here?" "Why?" "When do I need others, and when do I need to be alone?"

For me, living in the Possibility Space is always an adrenalin rush. I love the excitement, the energetic sense that I *must* do this, and the challenge of thinking through the details and structure of what I want to create. I need to sit in all of the seats on the merry-go-round. At work, if there's a need for a group space, I'm even more energized by sharing and planning through dialogue, mapping ideas and concepts, taking some issues off my list, or seeing others more clearly from both sides of the see-saw. Following reflection, I think best about new ideas when I'm talking. I create new constructs with each new conversation, and I'm always up for improvisation. I look for the feeling of moving forward, but I also need the reflection and mindful contemplation that leads to clarity. This is another example of the see-saw in my world.

## A FIRST-HAND EXPERIENCE

When I decided to become the director of the school that I headed up for eleven years, I was straight-out afraid. I'd had lots of jobs in education, but I had never been a building administrator. The first director of the school had not worked out well, and the superintendent was looking for someone new. I was helping out by checking with friends who I thought would do a great job for him, the staff and students. I gave him the names of a couple of colleagues to contact.

At that point, he said, "Elsie…I would like you to be the new director." There it was: fight/flight/freeze. I sat for a bit and didn't speak and then began to tell him all of the reasons why I shouldn't take the position. The conversation went on for a while. I asked for time and waited for a month. Talk about resistance. Finally, he refused to take no for an answer and said, with a huge smile and very convincingly, "There's nothing to worry about, Elsie. The busses come, the busses go. It's easy!"

Well…it wasn't easy, but it was exciting and more than engaging. You know, I had the opportunity to create a school. I used my experiences and beliefs about learning and leading, picked up new skills, and was able to challenge the status quo, design, build, influence, create, and improvise like crazy. The superintendent's belief in my ability to lead and to be creative was immeasurable over the years. The school was where I was supposed to be at the time. It was where

I discovered the true meaning of generativity—where I went to the edge of the playground and find what I thought were limits. I created new alternatives for action and new possibilities for the future. I checked my assumptions, raised good fundamental questions and asked myself, every year, what I was taking for granted. I was aware of the energy field in the school and was far more creative than I might have been in a very traditional school. There were many times during the years as I served the school and community that I felt resistance and heard the voices of judgment, cynicism and fear in my head, but I was more a creative leader in this role than in many others that I experienced over the years. Other opportunities to be a creative designer and leader had come to me earlier and were sometimes spectacular, but this one was special. Being generative IS being creative. I was glad I said, "Yes!"

My awareness of potential in that position was contagious. The staff joined in, and the school became a Possibility Space: the classrooms, the "gallery" where student artwork hung, the computer labs, science labs, couches in the lunch area, the spirit of exploration and learning. When I first began as director, I spent a considerable number of hours "dressing the stage" for what could happen there— art on the walls, colorful, engaging bulletin-boards, kites hanging in the halls and comfortable areas for the staff and students. It was a really different "container," and we worked hard to create a space where students could feel welcome and were encouraged to think and behave differently. They could consider possibilities for solving and creating problems that matter. More often than not it worked. There was always a field of energy in the building that was significantly positive because of our knowledge that we were focused on an optimal environment for natural learning: a generative learning experience. Guests would often tell us that they didn't want to leave… because they felt so good when they visited. The sense of openness and excitement about learning created a rich energetic space where we all learned and grew—where we lived. We sat in the seats on the merry-go-round, each understanding and accepting our preferences for where to begin, and we embraced the value of walking in the playground. We entered the Possibility Space together many, many times. It was a wonderful experience with creative leadership and learning, not only for me, but also for the staff, students and parents.

## PAYING ATTENTION TO THE UNKNOWN

I don't want to be a Pollyanna. The school experience wasn't always easy, and there were many times when we didn't have a clue where our intentions would go. We weren't always in control of outcomes. There was chaos and sometimes some good down-home disagreement. And sometimes the fear of not knowing what was coming next was overwhelming, but we kept going, no matter what. We confronted the resistance, talked, improvised, and looked at our work through different perspectives.

You'll need to be *mindful* of your reactions and responses to the Possibility Space and especially aware of the discomfort that can pop up there. Noticing your fears, reactions, and responses is essential, just as using your creative voice is essential. Taking a deep breath and stepping out to take action to create is what makes your work matter. Stepping out needs to be done, and it needs to be done by all of us—women who hold the perspective and initiative to create a new way of being for now and the future.

Go to your space—where you discover the piece of the puzzle that hasn't worked for you in the past and where you choose to create a wholeness of perspective to carry your ideas and intent forward. It's where possibility and the potential for a new order exist from very small to very large ideas and projects. It's where we are most afraid, because we don't know what will happen, and it's where we need to go more often. We're all artists. You *are* creativity and possibility, and this is where your journey begins and returns again and again. Your challenge is to find a journey that's worthy of you—where you can train your mind and fill your heart—a journey that will fully engage you as you develop your capacities as a creative being. You can all live in the Possibility Space: mind, body and soul. Remember: you must care about your work, your learning and your capacity to make a difference. Caring counts. You're the prototype. As Gandhi said, you must "…be the change you wish to see in the world…." Trusting the space and entering with gratitude for your creative capacity, your ideas and your intent will make a meaningful and significant difference. Inside-out: begin inside, take it outside. You're at the center of the design. How exciting!

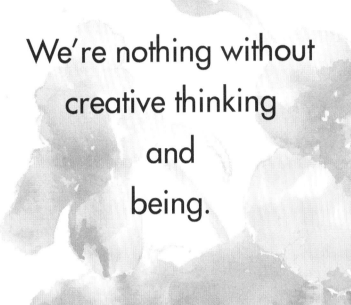

We're nothing without
creative thinking
and
being.

It's an *energetic*
connection.

CHAPTER 5

# INTEGRATING
# CREATIVITY
# PRINCIPLES

*Life and Leadership*

*There is only the dance.*

—T.S. Eliot

*I*f you're a creative leader, you lead from who you are. If you believe that you're a creative being and behave as if you're a creative being, your leadership will be authentic, meaningful, joyful, expansive and simply *better*. Creativity and innovation will be the heart and soul of your work. Your leadership comes from your passion, caring about relationships, joy and influencing others to think and be different. Yes, you pay attention to the bottom line, yet balance this with finding ways to invite your staff and colleagues to be keenly aware, powerfully imaginative and audaciously improvisational—to be emotionally and creatively engaged and involved. You see with new eyes, look for generative ways of being and thinking, take time to be silent and give time to your staff for reflection and original thinking. You influence your family, friends and colleagues to be courageous, disciplined, compassionate and mindful, and you influence them to take action. It begins with you. Your life and your leadership matter.

The graphic *Inside-Out: Building Your Creativity Muscle* has three principles for your guidance and consideration. They're all perspectives from women who are my life-long friends and colleagues. As I was preparing to write this book I trusted each of them implicitly to give me perspectives about creativity and leadership. The principles give you a foundation for building: for holding key ideas that are consistent throughout your life and work. Remember: We're nothing without creative thinking and being. These principles will give you a useful beginning.

## PRINCIPLE #1

# BE ORIGINAL AND STAND BY IT.

Sandra Johnson Packer
Former Art Teacher
Artist, Art Studio 7.5
Canal Winchester, Ohio

I wish I could paint like Sandra Johnson Packer does, but since I can't, I just surround myself with her work. I have lots of it. She's a powerful artist who's always trying a new medium or a new perspective. If you're interested, you can see her work on Facebook, since she puts it out there for the world to see, along with work from many other artists. I like her spirit, her courage and her talent, and I especially like visiting her studio where we talk about old times, and I buy her art. I met her in the 1960's when she was my younger sister's college roommate. She and I were at the same university for a year, and when I graduated we remained connected peripherally through my sister. Several years ago I found her paintings in a gallery in my hometown, bought a couple, we reconnected, and I visit her often when I go home.

When we talked, Sandy told me a story about a young boy who came to her studio with his parents and asked lots of questions about one of her large paintings hanging on the wall.

"Did you paint that?"

"Yes."

"Why would somebody pay so much money for it when they could just come here and look at it?" he asked.

At that question, she grabbed the opportunity to teach a bit, and they began talking about the difference between a studio and an art museum.

"How long did it take to paint that?" he then asked. "How much did the brushes cost?" "Why would you use different sized brushes?" "Can I buy this in a store?"

Good questions. In the end, Sandy told him, "If you go to a store like Kmart to buy a picture, you'll find prints, and there are more than one of the same." Of her piece, she said: "There is just one painting in this whole wide world that looks like this one. It's an original."

Sandy went on to say to me: "*This* is what I want to share. *Be original and stand by it.* We need women—and men—who understand that perspective."

We finished the conversation and went on our way.

Sandy says she gets hurt when she takes her art to a show. It's the vulnerability, like lying down on the sidewalk, unzipping her body from head to toe and waiting for the inevitable. Then someone buys a painting, and she's validated. I've used that image, as difficult to envision as it is, many times since she mentioned it. It's exactly what it feels like to take something original into the world. It's scary. And our resistance often keeps us from getting to the point where we create something that we want to share. Every painting that Sandy creates is an original. Every piece becomes a reflection of who she is, what she loves and how she likes to work. The essence of feminine energy gives meaning to her expression, intuition, originality, vulnerability and uniqueness. As women, we bring an instinctive life force to the universe, where our creative energy helps us birth new paradigms. We all need to remember not to step into a trap and submit to the status quo. Pay attention to the voice that lives inside. The "I can't *not* do this" voice. If you're afraid, that's normal. If you're not afraid, that's spectacular. Be courageous, positive and joyful about your reason to go forward. Have at it. Confront your resistance—your fearful and doubtful voice—and awaken your creative voice. Speak and act authentically. Begin...don't wait. Take your time and reflect about what you're creating. Get as many ideas on the page as possible, then choose those that work best. Be willing to improvise. And remember: the first few drafts are always awful. Being original means you're okay with that and can move into your Possibility Space with vigor. Be original and stand by it.

## PRINCIPLE #2

# *DANCE WITH THE DOG, AND THE DOG WILL DANCE WITH YOU.*

Catherine M. Neuhoff, Ph.D., Director
Butcher Educational Center
Warren Consolidated Schools
Warren, Michigan

Cathy Neuhoff, another artist and former art teacher friend who has been a public school administrator for around twenty-five years has two German shepherds, Emma and Charlie. She works with them in a training environment almost every weekend. When we were talking about creative leadership, she mentioned that she lives in the Possibility Space, where she can keep her mind open for opportunities. To do that, she tries to move into a mindful state—and she mentioned training the dogs. "Don't be angry when you're doing dog training," she said. "Dance with the dog, and the dog will dance with you." She went on to explain that when you're training dogs, you should be gentle with your approach. Have a deep knowledge of the dog and the task, use your intuition, be goal-oriented and purposeful, and be open-minded. Be perceptive. Learn what your dog can take. Be aware of the energy of both you and the dog. Be patient. Don't jerk the chain. When you drift off and aren't paying attention, that's avoidance. Breathe. This is subtle work. It's a dance. It's an energetic connection.

Do me a favor. Go back and read that paragraph again. This time focus on creative leadership. I'm not suggesting that people are like dogs, and neither is Cathy. I consider her to be a master of creative leadership. We're both suggesting that what happens as you work WITH the dog, who, like you, is a living system, is much like what happens when you lead creatively. Leading means thinking about *why* you do what you do, *what you do* and *how* you do it, along with how you might *improvise* and be *flexible* and *mindful*. You not only sit in all of the seats on the merry-go-round, but you also take a walk in the playground to get the big picture and understand what others feel and think when they're in those seats. Influencing others as a creative leader means that you need to *dance with the dog, and the dog will dance with you*. My daughter-in-law Rachel, who has worked with horses all her life, says the same. "Be aware of how the horse responds. When you're on the horse, there's an energetic connection—a communication. Sometimes you lead; sometimes the horse leads. You always learn what the horse needs and work with that." She tries to do the same thing with people.

Be aware of your creative self and where your creative being begins. Know that creative leadership is a non-linear path, and dance with your staff and colleagues. As a creative woman, you're smart, empathetic and able to dance. Use your own words if you must, but be sure to affirm your capacity to be flexible, gentle and intelligent— and creative. What would you do if you knew you couldn't fail? How will you nurture and hold a creative ethic in your professional life? How will you encourage others to awaken their creative voices and their passion? What will you do? Be sure to know where your voice will be heard and where you can make a difference. Know how to prime the pump and do the warmup. Then begin the dance, subtly, kindly and quickly. Be gentle, but be knowledgeable. There is only the dance.

PRINCIPLE #3

# *ALWAYS KEEP A SONG IN YOUR HEAD.*

Suzanne Culver
Former Peace Corps Volunteer and Teacher
Lancaster, Ohio

Suzanne Culver believes strongly about caring for others and learning about how others live and think. She's astutely aware of the need for different perspectives and positivity: the power of love in your life and for the people around you. We've been friends since high school. She and her husband Ken met while volunteering for the Peace Corps in the 1960's after they graduated from college. Suzanne is truly a unique friend, and I have great admiration for her pragmatic stance on life and work. She still sings with a women's group in Lancaster and volunteers at the local hospital, a choice that she says is like the Peace Corps. "You think you're going to help them [in the hospital], and they end up helping you." Suzanne mentioned the importance of interpersonal relationships in life, as well as the world of nature that we often never see. And she pointed out the value of music. Her question for me at the end of our interview was, "Don't you always have a song in your head?" *Don't you always feel positive about life?* It's a great question.

Be positive about yourself and your new ideas. Your job is to pay attention to what you *must* do. To act. So, say, "Yes." The negativity and fear of "I can't" will shut down motivation in a second. You must learn to tell the voices of judgment, cynicism, and fear in your head to give up and go away. Remember, they're just thoughts; they're the resistance. Then do something with your idea and open to the universe of possibility. Be sure to check how relaxed and alert you are at any given moment. Ask yourself, "How do I feel?", "How do I sound?", "How do I look?", "How do others respond to me?" Be aware of your resilience and to how open you are to experimentation and purposeful action. These are all indicators of your positivity and joy as a creative leader as well as a creative person. You will not be able to create from a negative mindset. You create from your joyful heart, mind, body and soul. I try to write Three Good Things that have happened to me within the last twenty-four hours in my journal every morning or evening, so that I can focus on positive thoughts. I also try to say "Thank you" as often as possible—to be grateful to others. It's amazing how impactful these practices can be.

By now you know that creativity is about play and discipline, emotion and technique. Be willing to improvise on the spot, but know what your structure must be. Think of the box of the context as a place to start, then change the context or create an entirely new one. Have fun and embrace joy. Laugh. Make a mistake and throw out the first draft or the first painting or the first plan. Do this with gusto. Be keenly aware that both a good sense of humor and being open and watchful within a situation are critical to your developing as a creative being. Always improvise...audaciously. Go to the park and watch the kids play. Better yet, get on the swings or the merry-go-round or the slide or TAKE A CRAZY FRIEND AND GET ON THE SEE-SAW!

*Always keep a song in your head.* Absorb the energy of playing and being open. There's nothing like it. It's astonishingly powerful.

Be authentic.

Have a courageous spirit.

Be in nature.

Awaken your
creative *voice*.

CHAPTER 6

# LIVING A
# CREATIVE LIFE

*Lessons Learned
and a Vision for the Future*

*Creativity is a shapechanger.*
*...a woman's creative ability is*
*her most valuable asset,*
*for it gives outwardly*
*and it feeds her inwardly at every level:*
*psychic, spiritual, mental,*
*emotive, and economic.*

—Clarissa Pincola Estés, Ph.D.,
*Women Who Run With the Wolves*

*A* note to me: Never settle. That's my motto. Be positive, proactive, creative and courageous. Live life as creatively as possible and allow creativity to change me. Know that creativity is my most valuable asset. Pretend that I'm under doctor's orders to be a woman who is fearless, who chooses to see clearly, and who will claim my own power…because, if I'm under doctor's orders, I'll pay attention. Be mindful. Ask myself, "Are you doing what you really think you're doing?" Breathe in. Breathe out. Breathe in. Breathe out. Smile.

## LESSONS LEARNED

There are many, many lessons that have come to me over the years, and I'm grateful, even though some of them were downright difficult. I'm sharing three of the big timeless ones, and giving them to you with a generous heart, with the hope that you can begin by knowing a bit more than I did when I started out, and that you'll work with these as part of your creativity muscle development. I'm seventy-two years old as I write this, so these are lessons from the grandmother, who hopes to be one of the wise elders in your life. If you're a reader near my age, I'm sure that you'll have lessons of your own to share. All of us have lessons. We all need to give them to others. Join in, in whatever way you wish, in your world. Lessons are valuable and help guide us, no matter what age we might be.

## BE AUTHENTIC

Once upon a time, many years ago, I was ready to become a school principal. This was during the early 1980's and much earlier than the goal actually became a reality with the school that I've described earlier. The job was in a small community near the lake: a charming, casual boating community, where everyone knew everyone. During the initial interviews in the summer, I watched videos of teachers teaching, answered the typical questions and visited the school, where

I met the secretary who brought her dog with her during the summer when the kids weren't there. (I loved that.) It all seemed to be a fit. I was very comfortable, and I seemed to connect well with those whom I met. I was invited back and eventually became one of two finalists. Although I was ready to be a creative leader, I wouldn't have called it that back then. When it came time for the final interview, I began to consider *what I thought I should be as a building principal*. I prepared what I wanted to say, but more importantly, I thought, I got ready for how I should appear as an "in charge" leader.

In this casual community, where I was having a final interview with the superintendent, members of the community, members of the board and one other principal, I wore a blue pinstriped suit, a white shirt, and a pin on the jacket lapel. I felt so business-like; until I sat down and realized that no one, and I mean no one, heard what I was saying. They were so astounded that I had dressed in a pinstriped suit that they really couldn't get past my appearance. That mistake cost me the job. I was told later that a dress with a jacket or sweater would have been more appropriate. The committee told the superintendent that they weren't comfortable with a person who didn't appear to "fit" into their casual community. *Interestingly, the pinstriped suit person that they saw wasn't me at all.* If I had been more authentic, I would have dressed differently and certainly would have been more approachable. I offered good answers to their questions, but it's hard—if not impossible—to be creative and inventive when you're not being yourself. The old adage "Perception is reality" was more than true in this case. I felt it during the interview, and I was absolutely right. I gave away my soul, because I was afraid that I wouldn't be perfect, *and* I didn't know how creative I really was. I'm very aware that this story may seem to be inconsequential and maybe even trivial to those of you who are reading today, but it was a great lesson then. The expensive suit went to the back of the closet, never to be worn again.

I didn't know about the see-saw or about the butterfly theory back then. During the 1970's and 1980's, when the feminist movement was in full bloom, many of us believed that command-and-control was the way to manage. We believed we needed to approach leadership with a more masculine stance. I used to think of us as pioneers. We didn't think about being creative, but we did think about being equal, and for many of us the awareness of our holistic capacity to lead wasn't fully developed nor was it discussed by feminists. During what I call my "early learning phase," I gave up who I really was and embraced a more masculine management style, believing that I would be more easily accepted and promoted. I was willing to move to the edge where I *thought* change could happen and consequently moved WAY OVER to the other side of the see-saw. But, I stayed there far too long, if I should have been there at all. I believe that women have always innately known that relationships, collaboration and compassion are at the heart of leading creatively. In the 21$^{st}$ century, where more of the "soft skills" are not only being acknowledged but are more consciously accepted, both men and women will need to find the balance of the see-saw.

I'm a woman who needs to continue to find and support her creative self, and, as I've mentioned earlier, I begin with silence. I try to be open to hearing my authentic and creative spirit. I've learned that this type of experience is what helps provide my power, just as it did for many of our Native American grandmothers. Entering the void from which all creativity springs is an ancient and powerful rite. When I become someone that I'm not, I risk losing my natural capacity to be creative. I give my creative soul away. In the long run, this is more than limiting; it's debilitating. I spend an inordinate amount of time trying to be what I think I need to be in a world that limits my true creativity. So I experience a loss of voice, power and influence: a loss of my feminine psyche. I lose generativity. I lose my home—my soul.

I encourage you to be hyper-careful to hold your essence as a creative woman. I've learned that excuses cloud the stream of creative thinking and being that flows throughout my life. I *can* get too distracted, *can* be resistant, *can* refuse to take responsibility for my work, and *can* find all kinds of reasons to choose not to be creative. Taking the time to see clearly and to know who I am and what I need and want is not only valuable, it's critical.

## TALK AND LISTEN WITH A COURAGEOUS SPIRIT

Through the years, I've practiced the art of holding nothing back. You know that feeling of not wanting to share because you fear being criticized or being treated as if you're too young or inconsequential to have a good idea. Most of us have experienced this at one time or another, and it's a killer for creativity and leadership. It's resistance and outright fear personified. Holding nothing back is bravery personified. I've learned to get my thinking and beliefs out there, say them with conviction, use my voice and be willing to sound silly or unknowing at times. Now and then I have flashbacks to when I was incredibly afraid of saying what I thought. I can still feel the fear. Each of us takes our work into the universe in a variety of ways, depending on the medium we choose and the context. My creativity shows up most often in leadership and facilitation. Talking and writing are my strategies for sharing, so I've worked hard to become more comfortable with not being perfect and not always knowing the right answer— or even the right question. I've learned to understand the power of talking together, of dialogue, healthy debate and good, insightful listening. Most recently, I've learned about the improvisational nature of conversation, and I find this very exciting. I've learned to use my creative voice in the moment and not wait until later.

I'm a huge fan of dialogue, and during my tenure at the school, I found conversations and focused dialogue to be at the hub of my creative leadership.

Holding authentic dialogue in settings where the conversation is *productive, interactive* (everyone has an opportunity to talk), where *relationships are developed, trustful feedback* is given, and there's *creative tension* between minding the store and free play helps lead to exploration and generation of new ideas and contexts. This happens in a one-on-one setting as well as with groups. Everyone exercises their creativity muscle. All styles and points of entry are welcome. Everyone is somewhere on the merry-go-round.

I begin with a question or a focus, wander around a bit, focus again, try new ideas, improvise, trust the unknown, get curious, spiral down to the essentials for this particular dialogue, refocus, come to closure. Sometimes we leave the talk and come back to it later after we have time to reflect. There's a spirit of both analytical rigor and inspired passion. Good listening is critical: listening both to others and to myself, to what I'm thinking and feeling. Being authentic and honest is critical: allowing vulnerability, mistakes in judgment, more than one perspective, as well as suspending judgment. For creative leaders, dialogue is hearing more than just "me"—and opening to the possibility of what "we" think. What do we believe? Where are our commitments? What are we excited and passionate about? It's the act of doing more than simply downloading my old mental models. It's opening to curiosity, the joy of discovery and relationships and trust between me and my colleagues. Dialogue can happen in a structured boardroom or staff meeting environment, or around the coffee pot in the lounge. Sometimes, the more informal the conversation, the more creative and productive the outcome will be. As the creative leader, I provide the container for interaction and energy, for trust and openness. I provide the opportunity to develop language and to use language that adequately speaks of our creative intent in ways that may be different from how we've talked in the past. I invite being different, subtly and gently. Then I invite action.

For more structured dialogues, I prefer working with circles or the council. These are ancient forms of gatherings that have drawn people together for respectful and meaningful dialogue for centuries. Sometimes my small staff and I would sit around a group of desks at the school; at my home the Women's Leadership Group gathers around the large dining room table. Open circles without tables are comfortable for forums or creative dialogues. Ordered Sharing is a form of very powerful circle dialogue that I learned from Geoffrey Caine and have used for many years. Whenever and however I "call" a circle, I am concerned about the energy that's generated among the group, the relationships that develop and the authenticity and creativity that arise and leave with each person.

As a creative leader, you'll want to find a structure that works for you, set agreements for the dialogue process and be sure that when the conversation is completed action is possible either alone or within the group. Since all conversations are improvisation, you'll not know, nor will anyone else, what will come from a good talk. We never do. I've found again and again that trying to control the outcome is both frustrating and a waste of my time. I look for awareness, attention/intention, openness, receptivity, sincerity and positive interaction. I always find some chaos in there, too. I don't tolerate cruelty. As long as curiosity and generosity of spirit are at the forefront, creativity will emerge. I just keep dancing with the dog, and I know the dog will dance with me—and with all of us.

## BEING IN NATURE

I've learned that there is great, expansive wonder in nature. It simply comforts me. There's the continuous nurturing of my body/mind/soul and an impressive example of how my living system melds with the living system that is the greater environment of earth, air, the sun, water and the moon. There is the nourishing, healthy energy of negative ions and the animals and birds that captivate me and who are my brothers and sisters. I go to the playground to play outside, where my creativity is alive and vibrant, and where I can laugh and shout and call to my friends or my children and grandchildren. I go to the woods for the quiet, silent, mysterious sense of fertile creativity—for connection to the earth—or to the seashore or lakeshore for the light, the sun, and the sound of the water that creates a sense of flow and timelessness within my being—the connection to air, fire and water. I see, feel, smell, taste and hear with heightened awareness. Creativity lives in nature, and nature lives in me. If I can be one with this environment, I can find the unified field of infinite possibility. I cannot be creative without being in nature. It's where I reset, allow myself to disappear and pay attention to life. It's where I most easily find the spirits of my ancestors and allies who guide me. As a creative leader, I've learned that holding retreats in a setting near the water, or near the woods or mountains, or in the Ohio hills near the caves provides a more positive, healthy and inspiring opportunity for creativity, dialogue and reflection. If I want to influence others to be more creative, settings in nature are the best containers around. They're the natural Possibility Spaces where my creative voice awakens.

## VISION FOR THE FUTURE

I learned many years ago that visions should be stated in present time so that they act as affirmations for where we wish to go. Consequently, we affirm: "I am," "We are," "(This organization) is." As we visit and revisit the vision, we learn to create and become what we've affirmed, and we can evaluate our progress based on our vision statement. The universe supports our intent, and we begin to co-create in a more enlightened and knowledgeable way. Here's a beginning vision that I have for you and me for the future:

*I am a creative, inspired, compassionate and joyful woman.*
*I use my creative voice with confidence and wisdom.*
*I know where my creative being begins.*

*I know my creative self.*
*I know where my creative leader lives inside of me.*
*I live in possibility.*
*I am keenly aware, powerfully imaginative*
*and audaciously improvisational.*

Now…you might consider this vision to be a bit too long, and I'd probably agree. But it's my vision, so I wanted to use my voice to give you choices. I'll most likely keep this in my journal and use it for priming the pump and affirming where I want to go in the future. We should always know where we want to go before we let go of where we are. Even though the unknown is always there, having a vision and intent for our lives is what sets the path for the universe to help us create. Co-creation doesn't happen only from the outside-in. So, if you find this too much for one thought or vision, feel free to choose parts of it. For example, you might want to focus on "I know my creative self." You might translate that into "I am a creative woman." Write this at least seven or eight times in your journal each day. Think about it over time…surround it with patience and awareness and love. Manifest it as part of your entire being. Visions are always about what you believe. They're also about where you choose to put your rich energy.

## IMPORTANT THOUGHTS

I offer you some important thoughts…for now: Step inside yourself with curiosity and compassion. Get to know who you are as a creative being. Go into the Possibility Space. Find your intuitive voice. Step outside with authenticity and confidence. Take along your intuitive insight and clarity. Use your creativity muscle with fire, gusto, mindfulness and perspective. Improvise with playfulness and focus. Gather other women together and talk, listen, learn. Take your creativity to work. Love your capacity to be a creative woman. *Awaken your creative voice.*

I'm excited for you. Enjoy the journey.

It's simple.

Energy needs you to be
open and *receptive*.

Then you start.

That's all.

CHAPTER 7

# JUST BEGIN

*Start. And then…ship.*
*Can't do the second*
*if you don't do the first.*

—Seth Godin,
*Poke the Box*

*B*eginning is the hardest task. Thinking about an idea, talking about it, visualizing it—all are part of the process. Beginning means stepping out and taking action, and it's scary.

When you're creating your own scenario in your own time and space, allow your creativity to unfold. Look at yourself mindfully, with focus and clarity. Develop compassion for your deep self. Step back. Become aware of your connection to the unified field, as if you were a bird within a flight pattern with a hundred other birds, all moving and flowing in the same direction. This is the energetic connection—the entrainment with other beings, and it is the adventure of a lifetime. I continue to practice focusing, allowing and recognizing that I hold a place within the energy field—the unified field. I cannot leave this to chance if I want to be creative. Natural emergence comes from this awareness and acceptance, as does infinite possibility.

When you enter the playground, at whatever point, and sit on the seats of the merry-go-round, focus only on what is happening in that moment, in that place. Try to think less about why you can't and more about why you CAN. Try to allow yourself to say, "Yes!" You'll engage both your mind and your heart along the way. That's how it must be.

Following are two scenarios that may help you see how to use your creativity muscle, along with some tips for beginning. The scenarios are working tools for you. They provide a picture of what you might consider under the circumstances that I describe, and may give you some sense of how to build your creativity muscle. The tips are quick thoughts that hopefully will catch your attention and stick in your mind and heart.

The first scenario is for personal development, the second for creative leadership. Both have elements in common, and both move from inside to outside and back inside again. I offer you the personal development scenario first, since I've long believed that we begin both change and creativity inside ourselves then offer them to others. However, I'm learning that within the energy field of the playground—which can be as large as you can imagine—influence comes from the collective consciousness of all sentient and non-sentient beings. We are all one. It's about us personally, but it's really about all of us collectively. The influence to co-create can come from any source, but you'll need to make the move to do the work and ship the results. First you must keep your heart open to your creative being. Then, you can walk on the playground and get on the swing, the see-saw and the merry-go-round. Go beyond the edges of the playground when you wish. You must also stop and reflect. Go inside, then outside—back and forth, again and again and again.

It's simple. Energy needs you to be open and receptive. Then you start. That's all.

## SCENARIO #1
# *PERSONAL DEVELOPMENT*

### CONTEXT

After a great deal of soul searching, you've decided that you wish to take a creative leadership role in your chosen field. There aren't many creative leaders in your arena. Most of the practices within your field are established, status-quo approaches, and you believe that it's time for some new thinking and behavior. You also believe that you are the person who can lead the way to more exploration, openness and generativity. You'll need to develop your technique and learn to be more systemic with how you proceed, but you're ready to be creative, energetic and viable. The time is now, and you are ready to go.

## USING YOUR CREATIVITY MUSCLE

TOOLS: Get a journal and a good pen that pleases you—that feels good in your hand and writes with a stroke that's authentic and assertive. Force yourself to write longhand, if you can. When you're writing and thinking, there is a correlation between what happens with your body and brain that's critical to creativity. Throughout this process, writing will be the first observable action that you take. I also keep a drawing pad close by to map or chart my thinking. If you're a visual thinker, this may be very helpful for you.

STEP 1: Begin with mindful meditation and reflection. Find a quiet place to sit or lie down. Close your eyes or keep them slightly open—your choice. Now just allow your breath to move in and out normally. Begin to pay attention to your breath and what's happening when your body breathes. What is happening with your feet? How do they feel on the floor or resting on the bed or mat? What is the level of energy in your ankles? Move your awareness from your feet and ankles to your calves, knees, thighs, pelvis, stomach, chest, shoulders, elbows, wrists and hands. Go slowly, continue to breathe comfortably and normally and allow your attention to move from the bottom of your body to your head. Focus on your neck, chin, cheeks, eyes, ears, forehead and crown. Be aware of the state of each part of your body as you breathe. Breathe in light and relaxation. Breathe out negativity and stress. Give your body/mind/soul the opportunity to be open, accepting and creative. Allow yourself to begin getting ready for change. Stay with this meditation for as long as you like. Simply continue to breathe consciously but normally. This is a practice for awareness. It's a practice that can be taken into the Possibility Space, where you can be aware of the unified field.

If you wish to write after the meditation and record reflections on the experience, feel free to write whatever comes to mind. Your intuition is likely to become more active and open after you meditate. Do this mindful meditation whenever you feel the need to retreat and breathe.

STEP 2: For this scenario, I suggest that you begin on the playground in any spot that you choose. I know that this seems less directive than you might like. Most of us want someone to tell us exactly where to begin. However, both your personal system and the larger system will begin to change when you step forward from what matters to *you*. So, ask yourself this question: *"What is my why?"* Why do you believe that being a creative leader at this point in time is critical? Why you? What matters to you? You won't begin, most likely, with wanting to solve every problem that you see in your arena nor will you be ready to develop a five-year-plan. At this point, begin where you are with what you know.

Spend some time journaling, drawing, talking, meditating and reflecting on why this intent to be a creative leader is so important for you. Walk around the playground. *Listen to your intuition.* What are you hearing or feeling? Write or perhaps share with a friend. *Look at the see-saw.* What is missing in your arena? Is there both a focus on detail and planning and a focus on people, emotions and joy? If not, what needs attention so that the see-saw is balanced? *How can you see yourself improvising*—acting in the moment to ask insightful questions, to encourage both yourself and your colleagues to play and take risks and to check your assumptions about the status quo? To rewrite their stories? To step into the unknown? To be willing to be wrong? To be vulnerable?

Through all of this questioning, you are being *mindful* so that you can achieve clarity and focus within your arena. Allow yourself to be aware and to be silent with what you see and hear. If you find it helpful, take your questions to work and watch what's happening there in real time. Gather as much information as possible, both inside and outside. Build your cache of information from all of the living system—your personal one and the one that exists around you.

*Stay on the playground until you're ready to begin creating. Then take a seat that seems most comfortable for you on the merry-go-round. Be authentic and honest. Where you begin is not an issue. How you begin makes all the difference. Just begin. You'll make your path as you walk on it.*

*Following are "Questions for Journaling" for each seat, which may help lead your reflection and action within your "why." There are quite a few, and they're presented in no special order. Feel free to choose questions that seem most appropriate and helpful, then move on to another seat when it's time. Be sure to sit in all of the seats. You won't create unless all seats have become a part of your process.*

STEP 3: Begin in the **Technique Seat** and pay attention to the details of the situation as you see it, as well as what you would do specifically to begin your personal development as a creative leader. This is what I call a "head seat" (meaning, more about thinking than emotion), and I see it on the left side of the see-saw.

### FOCUS QUESTION:

☞ *What might I consider as I begin developing my techniques and skills for creative leadership?*

### QUESTIONS FOR JOURNALING:

✍ *What are my beliefs about why change is needed? What grounds me in this seat?*

✍ *What are critical issues for change within my arena? For me personally?*

✍ *How do I define chaos, and how would I work with chaotic situations?*

✍ *Left to my own devices, what would I do if I had no other input?*

✍ *When I visualize myself as a creative leader, what do I see? What am I feeling? Doing?*

✍ *What skills do I possess that are strong, energetic and powerful for this journey?*

✍ *What might I need to learn to be more effective and creative? If I don't know what I need, who can help me?*

*Spend some time returning to your mindful meditation or go to the Possibility Space, where you can reflect, write, check your intuition, go inside to see what you feel you need to do and why you feel compelled to do this work personally and professionally. Simply slow down and take some time to allow yourself to build some space around the issue. Don't rush, and try not to resist. Try not to shy away from change that is beginning to happen for you.*

STEP 4: Go next to the **Play Seat.** You've been observing and playing with the situation and with your own perspectives and capacities for creative leadership. Now it's time to play a bit more. Some believe that play is the source of all creation. If that is true for you, beginning with this seat may be more comfortable than beginning with technique. You choose. This is a "heart seat," and I see it on the right side of the see-saw.

FOCUS QUESTION:

☛ *How might I engage my intuition, mindfulness and improvisation to allow myself to be more open, playful and creative?*

QUESTIONS FOR JOURNALING:

✍ *How can I encourage myself to observe more and make fewer judgments?*

✍ *How well do I collaborate and co-create? What opportunities am I ignoring or missing?*

✍ *What does this situation or my arena look like? Sound like? Taste like? Feel like? Smell like? How can I engage all of my senses more openly and joyfully through play?*

✍ *Do I have a song in my head? Can I write a song about this experience? Draw or paint it? Dance it? Do a theater improv just for myself?*

✍ *Am I really looking for possibilities?*

✍ *What is the energy around this change? Can I feel it?*

✍ *What does my intuition tell me?*

*Take time to reflect, visit the Possibility Space or do a mindful meditation, just as you did after exploring the Technique Seat. It's perfectly acceptable to slow down and take your time. You might want to talk about what you're discovering with a trusted friend or colleague. Listen to yourself. Pay attention to what you're saying and feeling. Then write more, if you wish.*

STEP 5: Let's go to the **Plan Seat,** just for fun. In the Plan Seat you'll want to do some analysis and look for a structure to anchor your work. Your journal may be the structure for your personal journey. In this seat you can use your imagination and generativity to design the plan. Shape your idea and play with graphs, charts, mind maps—whatever pleases you. Make them big, if you want. I use large chart paper when I'm planning and lots of circles, arrows, underlining and color. I have at least four charts for this book, along with many folders full of notes. Your charts and graphs may be more conservative, but do what you must to create a visual plan of your intended actions. This is a "head seat" and tends to be on the left side of the see-saw. Your planning process may take you to the center of the see-saw. Balancing head and heart while designing your plan is optimal behavior for creativity.

### FOCUS QUESTIONS:

☛ *What do I want to do?*

☛ *How can I be as creative as possible with my design or plan?*

### QUESTIONS FOR JOURNALING:

✍ *How might my planning process embody both my technique and my love for being creative and open?*

✍ *What do I see in my mind's eye?*

✍ *How can I design a visual that is enticing and clear for my proposed plan?*

✍ *Am I willing to try different patterns and possibilities?*

✍ *Where might I build in room for mistakes?*

✍ *Where does this plan offer high energy potential?*

✍ *How will I assess the effectiveness of the plan? How will I know if it's working?*

*Again…journaling, mindful meditation, walking, breathing, slowing down. Write, write, write. Walk away from your charts and come back to see them with new eyes. Stand in the Possibility Space to see what might come for you. Invite trusted friends or colleagues to tell you what they think. Be insightful and courageous. Be creative.*

STEP 6: Now to the **Risk Seat**. Here is where you allow your awareness to expand beyond the edge of the playground. Know that your brain and body/mind are uniquely yours. You will play with ideas that are clear in your mind and will find those that haven't shown up just yet. Fall into awareness of your energy and take time to connect with the unified field even more than in the previous seats. Take a chance. Be flexible. Like the Plan Seat, this will be a combination of head and heart. In this seat, allow your heart to be the leader.

### FOCUS QUESTION:

☛ *Am I willing to allow my creative being to come forward with freedom, joy and a good shout from my authentic, creative voice?*

### QUESTIONS FOR JOURNALING:

✍ *Am I open to rethinking and redesigning? Am I flexible?*

✍ *Am I filled with wonder and curiosity about how this change might make a difference in my life and my world?*

✍ *Am I committed to moving into my arena as a creative leader?*

✍ *Am I willing to make mistakes and learn from them? To fail forward?*

&#9998; *Can I learn to act in the moment—to improvise—and learn from the sense of focus and joyful freedom that comes with improvisation?*

&#9998; *Am I willing to enter the Possibility Space again and again to connect with "What if...?"*

&#9998; *Who needs to come along with me? Who can I invite to join the creative journey?*

&#9998; *If no others must come along, do I have deep courage and self-reliance? Can I go it alone?*

Once you've found a context for your creativity, have visited all of the seats on the merry-go-round, entered the Possibility Space many times, gone to the edges of the playground, written in your journal, designed your plan and talked with others about the passion and commitment that you have to move forward, you've *started* in a big way. You've been keenly aware, powerfully imaginative and audaciously improvisational. Now it's time to decide when to ship.

Ship is a word I learned from Seth Godin. I've used it for years now, and to me it means **Action**. You take your idea out into the world, send your plan to the CEO, publish your book, perform your dance or submit your painting for a jury review. *Then you begin again.*

You do your best to always follow the principles of developing your creativity muscle: *be original and stand by it, dance with the dog, and the dog will dance with you, and keep a song in your head*. The creative process is never-ending. You simply get better and better at being the creative being that you were born to be, and you join the unified field so that your natural creativity and ideas will emerge. How exciting is that?

SCENARIO #2

# CREATIVE LEADERSHIP

## CONTEXT

You are the leader of a corporate team that has been given an opportunity to design a plan to improve motivation and performance in your organization. For two months, meetings have been ongoing at several levels. When you're working with your team, the dialogue seems to be filled with ideas and promise for making improvements. There's a sense of openness and joy in the process. However, when you report progress at the corporate administrative level, your team's ideas seem to be met with smiles of indifference and questions that lead back to the status quo. The allocated time for reports at that level is short, and your work seems relegated to a spot on the agenda that holds no importance. After each report, you and your team are more discouraged but say you are still willing to hang in there—for now— even though there are signs of a loss of interest and energy around the issue. Personally, you're beginning to be agitated and angry and think that maybe you should make a meeting with the CEO to let her know exactly what you think of this assignment. But you don't shy away from a challenge or change, and you're very careful about giving away your power.

Something needs to be done differently.

## USING YOUR CREATIVITY MUSCLE

TOOLS: Bring out your journal, favorite pen and drawing pad, if you use one. These are the same tools used in Scenario #1. You'll be writing, drawing, thinking, and perhaps sharing through dialogue.

STEP 1: Begin with mindful meditation. Find a quiet place to sit or lie down. Close your eyes or keep them slightly open—your choice. Now just allow your breath to move in and out normally. Begin to pay attention to your breath and what's happening when your body breathes. Become aware of what happens in your nose—how the breath moves and what that feels like. Then the movement of the chest and belly when you're breathing. What is happening in your body, now, in this moment? What parts of your body are touching the chair or the bed or mat? Bring your thumb and your forefinger together on your right hand. How does it feel to touch your own skin? Develop your capacity for awareness through focus on the breath and your body, so that you embody the practice.

You'll find that your mind will interrupt, sometimes rudely and with no respect for your mindfulness practice. That's what your mind does. It thinks. When this happens, simply notice what you are thinking and move the thought to the side and out of the picture. Return to the breath. You'll do this again and again, no matter whether you've meditated for a lifetime or have just begun. This is what I mean by "removing the clouds." Watch the thoughts float by and return to the breath. Be in this moment for as long as you wish.

As in the personal development scenario, if you want to write after the meditation, feel free to put down whatever comes to mind. Remember that your intuition is likely to become more active and open after you meditate. Do this mindful meditation whenever you feel the need to retreat and breathe.

STEP 2: For this scenario, consciously begin in the **Play Seat** of the merry-go-round, where you collaborate, observe and discover. You're already in the Play Seat, since you've been doing this with your team for a couple of months now. In essence, you've been nurturing your colleagues and holding them in a safe place while they play with ideas and possibilities. You've also had a considerable amount of time to observe what happens at the board level. Be aware that your CEO doesn't owe you anything in this scenario. You co-create within the unified field to shape your space and your world. You never really create alone. Hold the awareness of being a creative woman and fight the tendency to feel helpless.

Take a look at the following questions. Find those that resonate with you and/or your team, then go inside by reflecting on the questions, and write the answers in your journal. (These are also questions for dialogue at the team level.) Here, again, there are a considerable number of questions for each seat. If there seem to be too many for beginning, choose what works best for you. Going deeper will be beneficial, but being willing to begin is critical.

## FOCUS QUESTION:

☛ *How do we optimize the opportunity for both collaboration and playing with ideas within the larger organization?*

## QUESTIONS FOR JOURNALING AND DIALOGUE:

✍ *What critical situation am I seeing (are we seeing) in this situation?*

✍ *What story am I bringing to this situation? What do I tell myself and others about what's happening here? Does my story have both positive and negative storylines?*

✍ *What do I need/want from this experience? How do I feel when I ask this question?*

✍ *Am I making assumptions? Do I need to look again?*

✍ *If so, how will I observe differently?*

✍ *Who are the people at the corporate level and where do they seem to sit on the merry-go-round? Are they able to hear my proposal? Where are they on the see-saw?*

*Pause. Reflect. Enter the Possibility Space alone or with your team. Slow down. Do a circle group if it seems appropriate. Ask yourselves, "What is happening so far? What are we learning? What perspectives are we bringing to this process?" Then take some quiet time to write and think about what is coming from each member of the team and from the energy field.*

STEP 3: Move to the **Technique Seat** to be sure that you are on target with the goals and details of the assignment. Check to assure that the skills and capacities of your team are appropriate for this task. Slow down and do the mindful meditation provided above or one of your own before moving to this seat. Ask yourself the following questions, and continue to write in your journal throughout this process.

## FOCUS QUESTION:

☛ *What skills or techniques might the organization need to begin seeing and thinking differently?*

## QUESTIONS FOR JOURNALING AND DIALOGUE:

✍ *What future situation do I/we want to create?*

✍ *Can we design a vision?*

✍ *How positive are we regarding the vision?*

✍ *Do we have the skills to change our stories if necessary? To see the situation through new eyes?*

✍ *How will I/we use the see-saw as a tool for expanding our perception of the whole situation? For knowing where our focus needs to be?*

✍ *What would others say about what I am seeing?*

✍ *What skills do I have to engage others in dialogue?*

STEP 4: Now to the **Plan Seat**. You may have a toolbox of charts or graphs or planning tools that work for you that help you see structure and help you analyze. You can find many of those online. Again, find time for silence and mindful meditation before beginning this phase. Use your journal to chart what you're seeing and how it impacts your thinking about the situation.

### FOCUS QUESTION:

☛ *What major tools, methods and processes do I have for reporting and planning that will catch the attention of the corporate board?*

### QUESTIONS FOR JOURNALING AND DIALOGUE:

✍ *When I/we draw, map or chart our perceptions, what do we see? Where are the workable and positive patterns and relationships? Where are the blocks?*

✍ *Where am I/are we stuck?*

✍ *What are our collective beliefs about change?*

✍ *Where are we seeing recycled visions, ideas and attitudes?*

✍ *What patterns or plans are emerging outside the parameters of our graphs and imposed planning visuals?*

✍ *Does this information inform our vision? Is our vision dynamic—moving forward?*

✍ *If we have not done so already, do we need to do an assessment of some sort? What do we __really__ want to know?*

*Take time for reflection and writing. Go to the Possibility Space. What possibilities are emerging? Sense the energy around your work. Is it at a low or high level? If it is low, what needs to be done? If it is high, what needs to be done?*

STEP 5: Now you will be ready for the **Risk Seat**. I hold this seat until last, because in this type of scenario, beginning with the Risk Seat is truly "risky." (Since you may choose to improvise here, be aware that doing improvisation publicly is frightening for some folks. Safe exercises for beginning improvisation can be found on my website: elsieritzenhein.com.)

This is the generative seat, where ideas, practices and opportunities begin to emerge more freely. It is also the seat where curiosity, fearlessness and self-discovery really begin to happen. In the Risk Seat, groups can begin to sense more clearly their cohesiveness and collaborative patterns. They will begin to self-organize more often than not. While you will have personal preferences about risking, including what you're able to do publicly, others will have different styles that may be more open or closed. It's important to be aware that everyone has a preference for where they're comfortable as creators, and that you'll need to acknowledge those preferences when you work with your team and the board. That said, along with the Play Seat, this seat is most often neglected in a creative group process, since it's the most frightening and the most challenging for most people. The creative leader steps lightly here but knows that without this seat, true creativity will not happen. Be sure to take time to meditate, be mindful of your scenario and of your body/mind/intuition when beginning this part of the process. Pay attention to all of them.

FOCUS QUESTIONS:

☞ *In what ways can I/we allow ourselves and others in the organization to experience being both relaxed and alert?*

☞ *How do I encourage information flow that is free both inside and outside the team/organization?*

QUESTIONS FOR JOURNALING AND DIALOGUE:

✍ *How comfortable am I with stepping into the unknown?*

✍ *How flexible are we as thinkers? (Can we dance with the dog?)*

✍ *How can I help others tap into the intelligence and creativity that exists within the entire organization?*

✍ *What generative questions do I need to ask to encourage creative risk-taking?*

✍ *How can I model improvisation and self-discovery?*

✍ *Am I comfortable with originality?*

✍ *How can I model "letting-go" so that new ideas and more creative solutions emerge?*

✍ *Who from my team will be my partner in this endeavor? How will we support each other as a team, especially when we feel vulnerable?*

EXIT QUESTIONS:

→ *What is our unique reason for being?*

→ *What are we really trying to accomplish?*

→ *How do we effectively meet our objectives?*

→ *What do we actually do?*

→ *What must we do differently?*

→ *When do we begin?*

(Adapted from *Generative Leadership*, 2008, p. 98)

## ENTERING THE POSSIBILITY SPACE

You've been given the task of coming up with a plan. All of the processes and questions that you've been working with throughout this scenario are part of Developing Your Creativity Muscle. You'll work from the inside out—always walking around the playground to explore your intuition, to stop for mindfulness, to check the see-saw for balance and to improvise. How you do this will depend on your personal intent and skills, along with the skills of your team and organization. You'll take what you experience and learn outside and return to the Possibility Space whenever it seems appropriate, so that you can connect with the unified field of energy and intent, where you can feel and see what emerges for you and your team.

When you reflect in this space, be sure to *allow*—give ideas and intuition a chance to emerge for you personally as well as for your team and the organization. This will feel strange, since it implies that you're stopping the momentum of the process. Actually, the opposite is true. Entering the Possibility Space allows the momentum to be enhanced by increased energy and love. Since all is unified and interconnected in this space, it adds integrity and purpose to our plans and creativity. You'll be able to step out with clear intent and desire to take action.

The **Exit Questions** provided above can help lead your reflection in the Possibility Space. You may not need them, but if you do, feel free to use one or two for mindful thought. Give yourself time in this space. Don't rush. Be sure to be aware of your intuition, your feelings and your emotion around the task at hand. Then tap into your skills and plans for taking action.

Finally, once again, the Action will be shipping—taking the plan to the board for report/approval or beginning again, if that's necessary. Moving the plan forward will be essential for change to happen.

The Beckhard-Harris change model describes that in order for change to occur, the following conditions must be met:

1. There is **DISSATISFACTION (D)** with the current state.

2. There is a clear and shared **VISION (V)** of a preferred future.

3. There are acceptable **FIRST STEPS (F)** to achieving the Vision.

4. The product of **D, V,** and **F** is greater than the existing **RESISTANCE (R)** to change among those whose support is required for successful implementation.

These conditions give rise to the following **CHANGE FORMULA:**

$$(D \times V \times F > R) = CHANGE$$

Your creativity and collective intent will be powerful forces in making change happen. Believe in it. Be aware of it. Love it. Use it.

## REMEMBER:

*Be original and stand by it.*
*Dance with the dog and the dog will dance with you.*
*Keep a song in your head.*

These principles are consistent throughout the process of developing your creativity muscle.

TIPS FOR BEGINNING

# *FACILITATING YOUR CREATIVE LIFE AND LEADERSHIP*

Facilitating yourself is about growing, developing and training yourself—but not about fixing yourself. You empower you. When you are in your power, your very essence has a different impact. You're part of the unified field, where emergence happens naturally. You're a generative, creative, joyful and loving being. You take the initiative. It's your idea, your choice, your action. Be full of courage and step towards positive action.

## HERE ARE SOME TIPS FOR BEGINNING:

1. Begin with questions: How do I feel about this idea? How can I see it differently? What must I do to make it better? Try your best to move from a reacting state to responding and listening.

2. Slow down. Be patient. Stay in receive mode.

3. Keep a journal and write your thoughts, ideas, maps, visuals… whatever comes that can take you to a different idea or concept. Write routinely, so that you can see your thoughts on paper.

4. We are all artists in our way. You don't have to paint or compose or dance. Put your ideas out there and create something for fun or be very serious and work with great intent. Your choice.

5. Go see or hear or experience art. Watch what artists do and allow yourself to immerse in their world. If you get a chance to talk to one of them personally, ask them about how they create… and why.

6. When you're at a meeting, write your notes in a different way on the paper. Slant the writing, put it only in the center of the paper, or write big. Allow yourself to feel how this takes you to a different place when you're in a context box.

7. Write a letter in your journal to the critic (resistance) that lives in your head. Give her a name. Welcome her to your world. Then tell her what you think about her interference in no uncertain terms, and tell her to back off and leave you to your good work. Be sure to write this down. Don't just say it in your head. Do this often.

8. Move. Walk, dance, run, exercise, do yoga or tai chi or swim. Your body needs to feel that it's involved with your creative life. Thank yourself for doing such good, healthy work, and then pay attention to what comes to your mind, heart and soul as a result.

9. If you don't routinely take time to be in nature, begin a good practice. Walk, sit, or do exercises outside. Breathe. Put your tongue on the roof of your mouth as you do this to facilitate the energy cycle within your body. Begin to feel your connection to the universe.

10. Say, "YES!" Say it again and again and again. Laugh if you mess up something, then begin....again. This takes practice. Be mindful and compassionate with your new life. Open up. Step into your Possibility Space. Find it and use it every day.

Enjoy!

# EPILOGUE

*T*here is much more to creativity, creative leadership and complex systems, of course. I've included a list for further reading so that you might continue your search, if you wish. Through the years there have been authors who were especially influential to my thinking and behavior as a creative woman and leader. Some are cited in the book, and others are included in the list for Further Reading. Among them are Clarissa Pincola Estés, Margaret Wheatley, C. Otto Scharmer, Peter Senge, John Kao, Jean Houston, Bill Spady and Seth Godin. You'll find similarities between my thoughts and models in this book and the U Process that's included in our book, *Generative Leadership: Shaping New Futures for Today's Schools* (2008). I believe the U Process that is described in great detail in Otto Scharmer's book, *Theory U* (2007), to be one of the most valuable models and processes for personal and organizational change that we have for this time. Also, Seth Godin is one of my favorite authors, speakers and marketing gurus. I read his blog every day. He doesn't waste words, and whether you agree with him or not, he'll make you think.

I decided not to include in-depth information and research from the neurosciences and education about the brain and creativity. You'll find a good discussion around these issues in *Generative Leadership*. The book includes a clear and focused view of generativity, living systems and brain/mind learning as a foundation for generative leadership in schools, as well as tools for dialogue and systems planning. We all know about schools; we all have an anchor there. Please feel free to transfer this knowledge to your business and organization, since it spans a much wider arena than education. I've also included resources on these topics.

Writing this book has been a joyful and insightful experience for me, especially with the help of my publisher, Kathy Mason, and her knowledgeable and skilled editorial staff and associates. I would also like to thank my son Rob for his patience, creative voice, and excellent photography and video production throughout the development of my website. This has been a fruitful exploration and a meaningful journey. I am most grateful to all who helped along the way.

Thank you, dear reader, for reading. Love and joy to you.

*For free creativity materials to support your implementation of the ideas I've presented, please visit:*

**www.elsieritzenhein.com/awakening-gifts**

# FURTHER READING

*I*f you wish to delve deeper, following are some suggestions for books and resources that may help you begin.

## CREATIVITY

Peter J. Denning & Robert Dunham: *The Innovator's Way* (2010)

Elizabeth Gilbert: *Big Magic/Creative Living Beyond Fear* (2015)

Maria Girsch, Phn.D. & Charlie Girsch, Phn.D: *Fanning the Creative Spirit* (1999)

Scott Barry Kaufman & Carolyn Gregoire: *Wired to Create* (2015)

Shaun McNiff: *Trust the Process* (1998)

Ken Robinson: *Out of Our Minds: Learning To Be Creative* (2001, updated 2011)

## INTUITION

Shakti Gawain: *Developing Intuition/Practical Guidance for Daily Life* (2000)

Judy Gee: *Intuition/Awakening Your Inner Guide* (1999)

## MINDFULNESS

Barry Boyce, ed.: *The Mindfulness Revolution* (2011)

Patty de Llosa: *The Practice of Presence* (2006)

Paul Wilson: *Finding the Quiet* (2009)

## MINDFULNESS AND CREATIVE LEADERSHIP

David Gelles: *Mindful Work* (2015)

Janice Marturano: *Finding the Space to Lead* (2014)

Sharon Salzberg: *Real Happiness at Work* (2014)

## MINDFULNESS IN THE CLASSROOM

Patricia A. Jennings: *Mindfulness for Teachers/Simple Skills for Peace and Productivity in the Classroom* (2015)

Daniel Rechtschaffen: *The Way of Mindful Education/Cultivating Well-Being in Teachers and Students* (2014)

Meena Srinivasan: *Teach Breathe Learn/Mindfulness In and Out of the Classroom* (2014)

## BOTH/AND: THE SEE-SAW

Otto Scharmer & Katrin Kaufer: *Leading from the Emerging Future/From Ego-System to Eco-System Economies* (2013)

Richard Sheridan: *Joy, Inc./How We Built a Workplace People Love* (2015)

Jon R. Katzenbach & Zia Khan: *Leading Outside the Lines* (2010) (This book is a specific discussion of both/and. It's quite clear and illuminating.)

## IMPROVISATION

Robert Lowe: *Improvisation, Inc./Harnessing Spontaneity to Engage People and Groups* (2000)

Stephen Nachmanovitch: *Free Play: Improvisation in Life and Art* (1990)

## EXPLORATION OF MIND-STRETCHING QUESTIONS

William Arnitz, Betsy Chasse & Mark Vincente: *What the Bleep Do We Know!?: Discovering the Endless Possibilities for Altering Your Everyday Reality* (2005)

# REFERENCES

Beckhard, R. in Bailey, S. (2000). *Making Progress Visible: Implementing Standards and Other Large Scale Change Initiatives/Visual Dialogue Tools with a System View.* Vacaville, CA: Bailey Alliance.

Caine, R.N. & Caine, G. (1991). *Making Connections: Teaching and the Human Brain.* Alexandria, VA: Association for Supervision and Curriculum Development.

Estés, C.P. (1992). *Women Who Run With the Wolves: Myths and Stories of the Wild Woman Archetype.* New York: Ballantine Books.

Gee, J. (1999). *Intuition: Awakening Your Inner Guide.* New York: Barnes & Noble.

Godin, S. (2011). *Poke the Box.* Do You Zoom, Inc.

Ibid. (2012) *The Icarus Deception: How High Will You Fly?* New York: Portfolio/Penguin.

Harvey, A. & Baring, A. (1996). *The Divine Feminine: Exploring the Feminine Face of God Around the World.* Berkeley, CA: Conari Press.

Houston, J. (2012). *The Wizard of Us: Transformational Lessons From Oz.* New York: Atria.

Jaworski, J. (2012). *Source: The Inner Path of Knowledge Creation.* San Francisco: Berrett-Koehler Publishers, Inc.

Jeffers, S. (1991). *Brother Eagle, Sister Sky: A Message from Chief Seattle.* New York: Dial Books.

Jones, D. (1999). *Everyday Creativity: Leader's Guide.* St. Paul, MN: Star Thrower Distribution Corporation.

Kao, J. (1996). *Jamming: The Art and Discipline of Business Creativity.* New York: Harper Business.

Klimek, K., Ritzenhein, E., & Sullivan, K.D. (2008). *Generative Leadership: Shaping New Futures for Today's Schools.* Thousand Oaks, CA: Corwin Press.

Langer, E.J. (2014). *Mindfulness.* Boston, MA: Da Capo Press.

Lowe, R. (2000). *Improvisation, Inc.: Harnessing Spontaneity to Engage People and Groups.* San Francisco: Jossey-Bass/Pfeiffer.

MacKenzie, G. (1996). *Orbiting the Giant Hairball: A Corporate Fool's Guide to Surviving with Grace.* New York: Viking/Penguin Group.

Pressfield, S. (2002). *The War of Art: Break Through the Blocks and Win Your Inner Creative Battles.* New York: Black Irish Entertainment, LLC. Roberts, K.R. (2014). Creativity Manifesto Blocks: DEMDACO.

Robinson, K. & Aronica, L. (2013). *Finding Your Element: How to Discover Your Talents and Passions and Transform Your Life.* New York: Viking. Romanovsky, R. "From Caution to Creation." Web blog post. The Creativity Post, 7 Oct, 2015. Web. 29 Dec. 2015.

Silverstein, S. (1996). *Falling Up.* New York: HarperCollins Publishers.

Taylor, M. (2008). *Daily Om: Inspirational Thoughts for a Happy, Healthy, and Fulfilling Day.* Carlsbad, CA: Hay House, Inc.

Tharp, T. (2003). *The Creative Habit: Learn It and Use It For Life.* New York: Simon & Schuster.

Wheatley, M.J. (1992). *Leadership and the New Science: Discovering Order in a Chaotic World.* San Francisco: Berrett-Koehler Publishers.

Wilson, P. (2009). *Finding the Quiet.* New York: Jeremy P. Tarcher/Penguin.

Zander, R.S. & Zander, B. (2000). *The Art of Possibility: Transforming Professional and Personal Life.* New York: Penguin.

# INSIDE ↔ OUT:

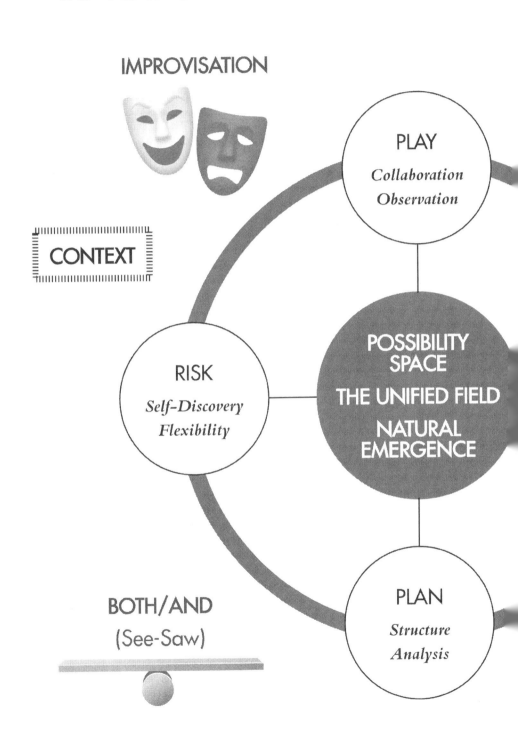

IMPROVISATION

CONTEXT

PLAY
*Collaboration*
*Observation*

RISK
*Self–Discovery*
*Flexibility*

POSSIBILITY
SPACE
THE UNIFIED FIELD
NATURAL
EMERGENCE

PLAN
*Structure*
*Analysis*

BOTH/AND
(See-Saw)

# BUILDING YOUR CREATIVITY MUSCLE

**INTUITION**

**BE...**

*KEENLY AWARE*

*POWERFULLY IMAGINATIVE*

*AUDACIOUSLY IMPROVISATIONAL*

**TECHNIQUE**

*Goals*
*Detail*

**PRINCIPLES**

Be original and stand by it.

Dance with the dog, and the dog will dance with you.

Keep a song in your head.

**MINDFULNESS**

**ACTION**

→ *Perform.*

→ *Ship.*

→ *Begin again.*

# ABOUT THE AUTHOR

Elsie Ritzenhein, Ed. Sp., is an author, speaker, and respected pioneer in leadership consulting. She delivers life-changing material to shift clients painlessly towards a new, more fulfilling future. She is a champion of instruction of Leadership Creativity Skills that offer remarkable insights to problem solving.

As a co-author of *Generative Leadership/Shaping New Futures for Today's Schools* (2008), Elsie has been engaged in a variety of educational roles for over fifty years. Her primary interest is generative thinking and action: developing the courage to challenge the status quo in positive, proactive and creative ways. Recent leadership initiatives include professional development for the Alliance for Academic Excellence, creating the Generative Leadership Women's Group, and developing Inside-Out, a program of intensives and retreats for personal and professional growth.

Through her personal growth and writing, she shares a deepening resolve to offer challenging, exciting and energizing possibilities to inspire women (and men) who wish to explore their innate creativity. Elsie feels that creativity is a lost art and wants to give current and future leaders creativity tools for problem solving the issues of today and the future.

Elsie is a grandmother and lives in Shelby Township, Michigan.

*Elsie would love to hear from readers!*
*Please email her at* elsie@elsieritzenhein.com.

*For futher resources, visit* www.elsieritzenhein.com.

Made in the USA
Lexington, KY
11 May 2017